CHRIST, THE CHURCH, AND THE END

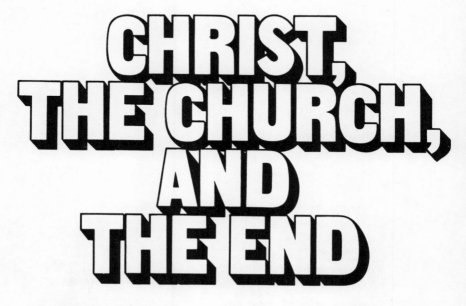

CHRIST, THE CHURCH, AND THE END

STUDIES IN COLOSSIANS AND EPHESIANS

JAMES M. EFIRD

Judson Press® Valley Forge

Christ, the Church, and the End
Copyright © 1980
Judson Press, Valley Forge, PA 19481

Unless otherwise indicated, Bible quotations in this volume are from *The Holy Bible*, King James Version.

Library of Congress Cataloging in Publication Data

Efird, James M.

    Christ, the church, and the end.

    Bibliography: p.
    1. Bible. N.T. Colossians—Criticism, interpretation, etc.   2. Bible. N.T. Ephesians—Criticism, interpretation, etc. I.   Title.
    BS2715.2.E33   227'.506   80-11781
    ISBN 0-8170-0862-4

In Honor and Loving Memory of
JAMES R. EFIRD
July 19, 1904—May 16, 1979

The Best DAD Ever

Preface

Having been invited to prepare a book which would primarily focus on the letters of Colossians and Ephesians but which would center on themes rather than exegesis proper, I began to meditate on these two epistles as well as on the period of the church from which they originated. It came to be more and more obvious that there were three basic themes contained in these two writings and that these same themes were prominent in the life and thought of the church at that time. It also became quite clear that the same problems which were troublesome for the church then are still today just as troublesome. Therefore, a study of the themes of the letters as well as the letters themselves is just as pertinent for today as it was for that era.

What were those themes which concerned the people of the early church so deeply? First of all there is the question of just how one understands the nature and function of Jesus the Messiah. In what way is he related to the church and to the members of the church? These questions lead naturally to a discussion of the nature and function of the church. And this set of questions leads one to consider the ultimate goal toward which the work of Christ and the witness of the church point. These three areas of concern have technical names in theological jargon: Christology (the study of the person and work of Christ), ecclesiology (the study of the nature and function of the church), and eschatology (the study of "last things").

These three areas of concentration are very prominent in the writings of the New Testament, and the interpretation of each of these areas remains contested (sometimes hotly so!) even today. For various historical reasons, which will be discussed later, the writings known as Colossians and Ephesians are specifically directed toward these three points. It is highly appropriate, therefore, for us to examine these two documents in order to ascertain what they have to say to the church today about these three important areas of Christian life and thought.

The basic method of presentation in this study will utilize the following outline. First, we shall examine something about the basic beliefs of the early church. Then there will be a *brief* discussion of each of the three areas, Christology, ecclesiology, and eschatology, to define the terms and to set the overall background for the fuller and more specific discussions of these teachings in the letters of Colossians and Ephesians.

At this point there will be a chapter dealing with the historical problems connected with the study of each of these writings. It is always of great assistance to the student of any biblical book to know as much as possible about the historical questions connected with the writing. Who wrote the book? When? Where? Why? To whom? Once one understands these issues as fully as one can, the teachings of the book become ever so much clearer. Some persons are turned off by these types of questions and investigations in spite of their value. If the reader wishes, therefore, to delay the reading of this chapter, the book is structured so that this can be done. But it would be very helpful and useful to come back to this chapter after reading the exposition of Colossians and Ephesians.

The final two chapters will consist of an exposition of the books of Colossians and Ephesians, and the reader is urged to use his or her Bible in conjunction with the study text given here. Space limitations do not permit us to print the entire text here, but it would be of infinite value to refer constantly to the biblical text. The reader will find in studying these two marvelous writings that there are several outstanding passages in each one, and it will become clear very soon that the basic problems and teachings lie in the areas of Christology, ecclesiology, and eschatology. This book is intended for the average church person who wants to learn more about Christ, the church, and the end.

As usual I would like to express my appreciation and gratitude to numerous people. To Mr. Harold L. Twiss, Managing Editor of the Book Department of Judson Press, go my sincere thanks for asking me to prepare this volume on these two marvelous New Testament documents. I would like to thank also those in his fine staff for their assistance and kindnesses in helping to bring this work to completion. Again and always I am indebted to my dear wife, Vivian, not only for her patience in typing the manuscript but also for her continuing encouragement and understanding with this project as well as in all of our life together.

And finally, if I may inject a very personal note, I would like to say a word about the one to whom this book is dedicated: my father. As I began to do the serious research necessary for the writing of such a book, he was stricken with a very serious and ultimately fatal malady. As I have said in the formal dedication, he was the best Dad ever, and I shall always be grateful to God for what my father has meant to me throughout my life. It is also quite fitting that a book focusing on Christology, ecclesiology, and eschatology be dedicated to him, for he was truly committed to the Lord of the church, he truly loved the church, and he has now experienced the final victory.

James M. Efird

Durham, North Carolina

Contents

Introduction

The goal of this book is to set before the average lay person a brief introduction to several key themes in the overall teaching of the New Testament books, the major emphases being the areas of teaching dealing with Christ, the church, and the end. In theological circles these are known as Christology, ecclesiology, and eschatology. It is not that these are the only three areas of New Testament teaching, but they are three of the most important and generate the most interest among Christian people today (and have done so throughout most of the history of the church). These three themes will be examined briefly, but the majority of the work will focus on two New Testament books, Colossians and Ephesians, for these two writings have much to teach us about these three emphases both generally and specifically.

To set the historical context in general, however, it is wise for the interpreter to have in mind some of the background for the early teachings of the first Christians. This background can help one to understand the early church and its teachings as well as assist in the interpretation of the New Testament writings.

As the early church had been born and began to grow in the light of Easter morning, the zeal and enthusiasm of its members gave momentum to the movement. This small band believed that God had done something momentous and unique in the history of the world. And they felt a compulsion to share this "good news." Therefore the early church came to be basically *kerygmatic* in nature. The term *kerygma* comes from the Greek word meaning "proclamation" or "preaching." The people who had been with Jesus in his life and death and who had experienced the resurrection had a message to proclaim—and proclaim it they did, with fervor!

Interpreters of the New Testament have been able by careful analysis of the New Testament documents to uncover what many believe to be the basic elements in the church's *kerygma,* or preaching. There appear to have been six points which were foundational for the faith of these people, and it is a real benefit for the student of the New Testament to keep these points constantly in mind. First of all, the early Christians appealed to the assurances of the Scriptures (the Old Testament was the only Scripture which they had) that a new age had been promised by God. That new age had, they believed, now dawned. This belief led naturally to the second point, namely, that this great event had been accomplished through the life-death-resurrection of Jesus of Nazareth. One must be aware that much more was involved in their thinking than simply the idea of the resurrection. While the resurrection was a most important element in the entire process, it was not simply the resurrection *per se* that was emphasized. The important point consisted in the identity of the one who was raised! Therefore the life of Jesus and the death of Jesus were emphasized by the early Christians almost as much as the fact of the resurrection.

Further (and this is the third point), the people of the earliest church believed that Jesus had been exalted to the right hand of God as head of the New Israel. The early church did not view itself as a new entity but as the legitimate continuation of the Old Israel of God. The Christians had now become the elected body called to be the instrument through which the name of God would be made known in all the world. Jesus' elevation to the right hand of God connoted for these people a unique significance and authority for their leader, to whom they had now committed their lives. Even though Jesus was at the right hand of God, they believed nevertheless that his Presence was still with them. The evidence for this further (and fourth) point could be demonstrated through the work of the Spirit (the Holy Spirit) which was being manifested within the church and among the people of the church. The early church believed that the Spirit had been sent to them as a gift of God and as a potent reminder that Jesus was still active among his followers (see especially John 15–16).

One of the most cherished beliefs (and one which even today carries great emotional weight) was that Jesus was going to return *soon* to consummate the kingdom. The technical term for this return among New Testament scholars is *Parousia,* from the Greek word meaning "coming" or "presence." The early Christians believed quite strongly that this momentous event would occur *within their lifetime.* For example, in several of Paul's earlier letters, it was considered quite unlikely that anyone would die before the Parousia. The fact that people were dying caused some very real consternation among some of the church people of that era (see 1 Thessalonians 4:13ff.). The imminent return of Jesus was a dominating force in the thinking of the early church (see 1 Corinthians 7:26ff.). This belief in the Parousia constituted point five.

The final aspect of the kerygmatic proclamation of the early church was, as one would probably guess, an urgent appeal for any hearers to respond positively to the act of God in Jesus and to accept the new life being offered and made available to all people. As is well known, numbers of people did indeed respond positively to this zealous appeal. One should not be misled at this point, however. Many church people through the years have thought that the church grew by huge multitudes accepting the new faith wherever it was proclaimed. The very large and early success at Jerusalem upon which this idea is based (see Acts 2) was the exception, however, rather than the rule. When one encounters church meetings in the New Testament, one finds that these groups were relatively small, the members able to meet in someone's house. And homes were not nearly as large then as they are today!

These six points, therefore, seem to have been basic to the proclamation and belief of the earliest Christians. It was natural that as the church continued to grow, develop, and as time (inevitably) marched onward, certain points began to be refined, expanded, and some even modified. As the apostolic age (the period of time during which most of the apostles were still alive) became the post-apostolic age (the period during which the church began its second generation apart from the eyewitnesses of the events surrounding Jesus the Messiah), the three basic points which we are considering seem to have been at the center of the church's thinking. Naturally the ideas associated with Jesus were developing. It was not enough simply to say that Jesus was "Son of God" or to confess "Jesus is Lord." What did these terms mean, and what significance could be attached to Jesus' unique relationship with God?

A second matter of major concern was directly associated with the belief in the early return of Jesus. The church had believed strongly that the Parousia was near, but it had simply not come to pass. As the first generation became the second and the second the third, it became obvious that some rethinking of that doctrine had to be done. And various New Testament books written in the post-apostolic age (i.e., after about A.D. 70) attempted to give answers (either directly or by implication) to the problems that the delay in the Parousia caused.

Closely related to that issue was another. Since the early church believed that the Parousia would take place soon, within its generation, there had been no real organizational structure and no real planning for the future. What organization there was seemed to be mainly an *ad hoc* arrangement which dealt with whatever specific problem(s) an individual church might have at any given time. There were no real "political" offices in the church. If indeed the Parousia were coming soon, there could be no need of structure or planning. These matters were largely ignored. But finally it became increasingly clear that the church was in for a long period of struggle with the world. How was it to face these new challenges over a "long haul"? What kind of structure would help the church to maintain its identity and purity? What kind of leadership would be needed now that the apostles and eyewitnesses were no longer present?

It is exceedingly important to keep all these matters in mind when studying the New Testament, but it is particularly important when one comes to study the two writings to be considered here: Colossians and Ephesians. These are important books in precisely the three areas which were and still are so crucial to a proper understanding of the Christian faith.

There is some serious debate about the dating and authorship of these writings. Some argue that both are by Paul and to be dated about A.D. 60-64. Others argue that neither is by Paul and both are to be dated in the latter part of the first century A.D. Still others argue that Paul authored Colossians approximately A.D. 60-62 and a later admirer of Paul wrote Ephesians near the end of the first century A.D. No matter which of these solutions is chosen, it is still clear that both books reflect the church's thinking near the end of the apostolic age and at the beginning of (if not actually later into) the post-apostolic period.

The dating of the books is of primary importance, and these matters will be discussed more fully later (see pp. 41-52).

These two letters, therefore, are of primary importance not simply for the times in which they were written but for the church in every generation. Each new group of Christians is forced to examine anew these same questions: Who is this Jesus and why is he significant? What exactly is the nature of the church and how do its members relate to each other and to the world? How does one interpret the New Testament teachings about the "end"?

The purpose of this short study is to examine how the New Testament in general gave answer to these questions and to examine in some detail the specific and significant answers to these same questions as explicated in the writings known as Colossians and Ephesians.

1

The Person and
Work of Jesus

It is not to be assumed that these three motifs—
Christology, ecclesiology, and eschatology—are the only ones found
either in Colossians and Ephesians or in the other New Testament
books. Far from it, but it is true that these three find a "pride of place"
among all the other doctrines. Christology may be defined as the
discussion concerning the Person (nature) of Jesus and what Jesus
accomplished (his work), ecclesiology as the discussion about the
nature and mission of the church, and eschatology as the discussion
about "last things." It is interesting to note that these three areas are
precisely the areas which have triggered the most hotly debated
controversies in the history of Christianity, and they still today are
subjects of intense study and discussion. It would certainly seem to be
in order to discuss briefly these three areas as they were debated in
New Testament times to ascertain if the struggles and understanding
of the New Testament writers still speak to the church today in these
vital areas.

The first of these areas to be examined, by order of priority, must
be that concerning the figure of Jesus the Messiah. Without the figure
of Jesus there would have been no church and no eschatology in the
Christian sense. There have always been some persons who have
attempted to dispense with Jesus as the central figure in Christianity,
but the fact is that without Jesus, there is no Christianity! One may or
may not like this point, but it is basic to the understanding of the New
Testament faith and the Christian faith today.

From the very beginning of Jesus' ministry those who came into
contact with him realized that here was no ordinary person. Not only
his followers sensed this, but also his adversaries. One does not plot to
remove permanently a person whose existence is not a distinct and

real threat to one's own well-being. His enemies came to the conclusion that the only way to deal with him was to kill him! Neither they nor even Jesus' disciples, however, realized just who it was with whom they had come into such intimate contact. The enemies felt that they could kill him and be done with him; his own followers felt that with his death the movement he had come to inaugurate was finished.

Following Jesus' resurrection from the dead, the disciples at least began to understand a bit more fully some of the teachings he had given to them during his lifetime. But even then, they had not fully understood the depth of his being. They realized that he was a special and unique person, and they attempted to explain his person and work in terms which they and others in the early church could understand. It took the church until the Council of Chalcedon (A.D. 451) to finalize a statement for all Christians which related to the person of Jesus. These church fathers acknowledged the uniqueness of Jesus and laid down the formulation that he was two natures (divine and human) combined into one Person. This was considered a mystery, yea, even a miracle—the miracle of the incarnation. From that time the concept of two natures in one Person has been "orthodox" Christology.

Some of the church fathers' thinking was based on the New Testament teachings which were called forth by specific historical circumstances, such as those in the background of Colossians and Ephesians. It has not been recognized as often or as readily as it should have been that much of the New Testament teaching about Jesus arose from concrete historical problems encountered by the early church, and that these problems were quite often answered by means of metaphors or figures of speech appropriate for dealing with these specific problems. What can one make of these passages and teachings now? And can we rely upon them as definitive for our time and our understanding of the Christ? Is it legitimate to take figures of speech and make philosophical "realities" of them? How can we today understand this Person without whom there can be no Christian church?

The answer to those questions is not easy to find. Perhaps the best way to approach these matters is to look briefly at the various ways the early church, as reflected in the New Testament writings, attempted to distinguish this unique individual. The early church understood that Jesus was, in a unique way, "Son of God." That term had been applied to other persons in Old Testament times (such as the king), however, and the early followers recognized that this was not enough to describe the Person whom they had come to know. The term which was early utilized came to be that of "Lord." In the Old Testament times the various gods of the nations had individual names, and the God of the Hebrew people also had a name. As nearly as we can determine, that name was *Yahweh*. Since the Hebrew language had no vowels, the name contained four consonants, and hence is referred to as the "tetragrammaton" (the "four letters"). This "name" was believed to be so special and unique that to use the name in anything other than the most proper way was to court disaster. Therefore, the word itself came to be viewed as so sacred that it could not even be pronounced; and wherever the word occurred in the sacred writings, it was pronounced *Adonai*, which was the Hebrew word for "master, lord."

By the time the Septuagint (the Greek version of the Hebrew Old Testament) was translated, it was common for the Greek word *kurios*, "lord," to be used for the tetragrammaton. It should also be noted that in the Greco-Roman world the word *kurios* was used for some of the gods of the ancient world. Therefore, the term *kurios* was well known, recognized as being a term referring to the world of deity, and suitable for use in describing Jesus to the world! Thus the earliest Christian confession was "Jesus is Lord." This was an exceedingly high designation for Jesus since identification of anyone with the God of the Hebrews was unthinkable in Jewish circles.

Since the early church believed that Jesus was the fulfillment of the Old Testament hopes and that Jesus was somehow uniquely related to God so as to be called "Lord," the people of the church looked for other parallels in their Scriptures by which Jesus could be defined or described. They naturally believed that he was the Messiah (the Christ); and since Jesus came from the lineage of David, much was made of that connection. Further, there was a very strong emphasis on Jesus as the Suffering Servant. The Servant passages are found in Isaiah 40–55, the major and best-known of them being Isaiah 52:13–53:12. One can easily determine from reading the Gospel of Mark, for example, that Jesus was interpreted in light of these passages (even though these passages were not at that time considered "messianic"). Other indications of this connection may be found in Acts 8:26-35 and in the writings of Paul, especially in the christological hymn found in Philippians 2:5-11 (see especially 2:7).

Another emphasis made in the early church seems to have revolved around the idea of Jesus as *the* prophet (see Acts 3:22ff. and Acts

7:37), but this does not seem to have been nearly so pervasive as some others. A further interpretation depicted Jesus as the new or second "Adam." As Adam was the first human and the founder of those who have rebelled against God, Jesus is the new Adam or the new "man" who is the founder of those who have been reconciled to God and have had their old humanity transformed into a new humanity. One sees this in Paul quite frequently (see Romans 5:12ff.; 1 Corinthians 15:22, 45ff.).

Another favorite comparison was made between Jesus and the "stones" of the Old Testament. These stones were keystones which held buildings together (Psalm 118:22) or cornerstones upon which foundations were laid (Isaiah 28:16) or perhaps even the stone of Daniel 2:34ff., which was "cut out by no human hand." These figures are found in various New Testament books (see especially 1 Peter 2:4-8; Acts 4:11), and this idea will be specifically studied in considering Ephesians 2:20-21.

One sees in these attempts to explain Jesus a Christology which emphasized the *work* of Jesus more than it emphasized the *nature* of Jesus. This was not because the people of the early church viewed the person of Christ as less important than the work of Christ, but rather it was because in their experience they could speak of what Christ had done and had meant to them much more specifically than they could discuss the philosophical niceties of "being." Therefore, in the discussion here, as in the New Testament itself, the emphasis will also be on the work of Christ. This approach will not neglect the questions about the nature of the person of Jesus; that kind of thinking, however, actually emerged later in the history of the church.

For the sake of simplicity, our discussion will center on three aspects (primary ones) of Jesus' work: revelation, reconciliation, and resurrection. These three aspects are crucial to the understanding of the church's proclamation of and experience with the risen Lord, and they are central in the books specifically under discussion here. One must beware, however, of attempting to separate these items into single, self-contained categories. Each is part of the larger whole which constitutes the early church's understanding of Jesus' person and work.

First, and most importantly, Jesus was understood as the one whose basic function was to reveal God to the human race. The Old Testament taught clearly that no one could look upon God, but the New Testament writers believed that in and through the Person of Jesus of Nazareth one could see in human form what God was like.

This did not mean, of course, that Jesus was a photographic image of God, but rather they believed that to look at Jesus' life and person and actions was to see what God would be like. And more importantly, persons could see what human beings *ought* to be like. When one thinks about the revelation of God to humanity, it becomes clear that there can be no higher revelation of God given to the world than one given in terms of a human personality.

The prologue to the Gospel of John (John 1:1-18) probably says this as clearly as any New Testament passage. ". . . we have beheld his glory, glory as of the only Son from the Father. . . . And from his fulness have we all received, grace upon grace. . . . No one has ever seen God; the only Son [some texts read "God" here], who is in the bosom of the Father, he has made him known" (John 1:14-18). The word used in the Greek and translated "made [him] known" really means "to lead the way," thence "to draw out the inner meaning." (It is the word from which we get the English word "exegesis," which means to draw out the real or inner meaning of a text.) Jesus, therefore, was interpreted to be the unique revelation of God.

In Colossians Jesus is called the "image of God" (see Colossians 1:15). And while this particular figure is debated among scholars, it seems clear from the text that Paul intends here to give the meaning of "revealing" God to the world. This was his function, his work to perform. Now to be able to do this, Jesus had to be a very special and unique person. And this special and unique person did not become such ordinarily, but only because in him the "whole fulness of deity dwells bodily" (Colossians 2:9). But the emphasis here, while reflecting on Jesus' nature, is primarily concerned with the purpose of God. All that happened was for the purpose of people coming "to fulness of life in him" (Colossians 2:10).

The revelation of God, given to the world in and through the person of Jesus, has as its basic goal something far beyond a simple "revealing" of what God is like. God's revelation is always for a purpose. The revelation is unique because the purpose is unique.

This leads to the second consideration, that of a teaching which is quite prevalent in Paul's writings and in Ephesians as well. This relates to the basic understanding of Jesus' work, namely, reconciliation. Many persons through the years of church history have understood Jesus' work, specifically as it is centered in the cross, as a work viewed in the legalistic sense. One recalls the image which is so popular of the guilty sinner called before God's court of judgment and pronounced "not guilty" because of God's act in Christ.

This view is based upon the old idea of God's honor, justice, purity, righteousness, etc., being violated. God is therefore angry, and the guilty sinner deserves to die. But in the cross Jesus "took the blow" that was intended rightfully for each human being. If one reads the writings of Paul carefully, however, it can be clearly seen that this is not really what Paul is saying. In the first place, Paul never argues that human beings can be pronounced "not guilty." This would be a violation of God's basic honesty and righteousness; and further, such an interpretation places the emphasis on what Jesus did as primarily done for the benefit of God, whereas Paul always emphasizes that the act of God in Christ was done for the benefit of the world. The fact is that what happened in the act of God in Christ cannot really be fully understood, but at its base the idea is that of forgiveness. God has simply forgiven the sin of the one who has accepted the benefits of God's fullest revelation and has committed oneself to God in Christ. A new relationship has been established.

This new relationship is most usually designated by the term "reconciliation." The most famous passage where that idea is found is 2 Corinthians 5:16-21. But the same teaching is also located in Colossians 1:18 and Ephesians 2:16. And the emphasis on the forgiveness of sins is found in both Colossians 1:14 and Ephesians 1:7.

What the teaching appears to be, simply put, is that of a situation where two persons are angry with each other. They are not in the right and proper relationship. They need to be reconciled. But what if one party is ready, willing, and able to forgive and to resume a positive relationship with the other? Who is it that needs to be reconciled? The one who is ready and willing to forgive and to begin anew? No! The one who is still angry and estranged. According to these teachings something like this has taken place in the relationship between God and the human race. God is ready to forgive, and through the life-death-resurrection of Jesus he has done something very positive. He has made it possible for human beings to become reconciled to God. They cannot do it by themselves. But somehow, inexplicably, through the cross something has happened which reconciles not only human beings but also the entire world to God. The one who does not need to be reconciled has made it possible for the one who does to become reconciled. It is a great mystery which needs to be accepted, not simply defined and debated.

This reconciliation which leads to a new relationship with God points toward the last of our discussion points. What God accomplished through the work of Jesus had culminated in Jesus' resurrection. Exactly what happened in the resurrection was not known to the New Testament writers. Each one seems to explain it and the events surrounding it in a somewhat different way. But of one thing they are all absolutely certain. Jesus was raised! Again the most important matter to the New Testament church seems to have been the meaning of this stupendous event. Exactly what happened was not so important as that it happened and what that signified.

To Jesus it signified one thing—new life, a new beginning. And with that new life there was made available for all those who would follow him a new life of their own. We shall shortly discover how very important it was to the authors of Colossians and Ephesians for Christian people to behave and to act differently from the old world from which they were called. There are numerous passages in both writings which testify strongly to that (see   Colossians 3:5-17; Ephesians 4:17-5:20). And in almost all of the New Testament writings there is a clarion call for a new life, freed from the sins of the world.

Therefore, the great work of God in Christ culminated in the giving of new life to the world. This life was a gift, freely given, and the recipients were truly unworthy. But God in his mercy, love, and righteousness had done something for the world which it could not do for itself. And in accepting this great gift the person was called into a position of communion with God and fellowship with other persons similarly called and committed so that this word of reconciliation could go out to all the world. Because it was intended for all the world!

In the New Testament writings one can clearly see that the emphasis in the teachings about Jesus centers on his work rather than on his person. This is not to say that these writers were always thinking about a "functional" Christology as some scholars have argued. It is simply that they could understand more clearly and precisely what Christ meant in their lives and in their world, while also recognizing that here was a Being unique in that he was related to God in a special way that others were not and could not be. Through the centuries of church history the emphasis of the church has been centered far too often on who Jesus was rather than what Jesus did. And the two cannot really be separated, for neither dimension can exist apart from the other.

Perhaps what the church needs to do is to rekindle again the emphasis of the New Testament writers who, such as the two we shall study in this book, can affirm that in Jesus the whole fullness of God dwelt bodily. And in so doing he has brought us a revelation of God which emphasizes that reconciliation can now become a reality between God and the world. And through that revelation and reconciliation the entire universe can have new life. Perhaps what we need is a recommitment toward understanding the work of Christ—while not disparaging the person of Christ—to allow the Spirit to be active in the church to complete the work begun in Christ. This is a real challenge for the church.

2

The Structure and Nature of the Church

As one would well imagine, there was no set or formal structure within the early church. The reason for this was at least twofold. No one really has a plan of organization for a movement that has just begun and that rather abruptly. But even more importantly to the people in the early church, the belief that Jesus was to return shortly seemed to militate against the need for any structure. The time was short, too short to be wasted on organization and structure.

But that type of thinking soon collided with the reality that even if the Parousia were near, certain daily duties needed to be performed until that momentous event happened. The first record of such an experience is given in Acts 6:1ff. Certain widows were being neglected in the "daily distribution" which caused some dissension among the church members. The problem was that the church looked to the "Twelve" to handle all church matters, but the church had grown to the point that even in this early time certain duties had to be distributed and delegated to others.

This episode also reflects the central importance in the early church of the "Twelve." Some refer to this group as the "apostolate," but it is clear from the New Testament writings that the "apostles" were not limited simply to the Twelve. Naturally that group was afforded primary respect and deference because these were the ones who had been with Jesus from the beginning and who had seen the risen Lord. There is, however, some strong evidence from the New Testament documents that the term "apostle" was not limited to that small group, nor simply to those who had been with Jesus from "the beginning." Paul himself is called an apostle, and he uses the word in his letters in a manner that suggests that there were more "apostles" than the Twelve (see, for example, 2 Corinthians 8:23; 11:13; 1 Thessalonians 2:6; 1 Corinthians 15:7; and others).

It is interesting to note in this connection that there is the possibility that there may have been a female "apostle"! In Romans 16:7 Paul says, "Greet Andronicus and Junias . . . men of note among the apostles." It has been assumed for many centuries that Junias was a male, but there is the possibility that the word in Greek could refer to a woman just as well. In fact the oldest Greek manuscript of Paul's letters (called P 46) definitely reads "Julia" at this point. It is easy to see how the later scribes would understand apostles as masculine and change the text to read that way. It is less understandable to explain the change from the masculine to the feminine, and therefore the feminine reading may well have been the original. Remembering the prominent place which certain women played in some of Paul's churches (Priscilla, for example, in both Corinth and Ephesus), it would not be surprising for Paul to think of women as apostles if the term did not refer explicitly and solely to the Twelve.

From the earlier New Testament writings it appears that most of the organization and structure of the church was rooted in the church's needs. Each person in the church was looked upon as having a "gift" which was to be used for the strengthening and building up of the entire group. This type of situation is clearly seen in 1 Corinthians 12.

But as any organization or institution grows and develops, there arises a need for persons who are charged with responsibility for making certain that the affairs of the group are properly managed. And ultimately this happened in the development of the Christian church. Exactly how this occurred or when is not as evident as we should like it to be. It appears that the church developed leaders because of the current needs of each congregational group. And it is not at all certain that the different names for the leaders (such as overseer, elder, deacon) referred to the same tasks in all the churches.

There were "elders" who seem to have played a prominent part in the book of Acts (see Acts 11:30; 14:23; 20:17ff.), but it is interesting that these are not mentioned in Paul's writings. They are mentioned in First Timothy (see 5:1, 17, 19) and Titus (1:5); the author of Second and Third John calls himself "the elder," and the book of Revelation used the term as one of its many figures. Exactly what the "elder" did is not really known, but it appears that the term denoted a person of some standing and authority in the church structure. It is possible that the term "elder" arose from the Jewish background (for there were "elders" among the Jews); and when the church spread in the Gentile world, these came to be known as "overseers" [Greek *episcopos*] (see Acts 20:28).

The additional term, therefore, used in the church was that of *episcopos,* "overseer," from which we obtain the term "bishop." But the *episcopos* of that time was far different from the office as that developed in the history of the church. The word *episcopos* is used very infrequently in the New Testament (Philippians 1:1; 1 Timothy 3:2; Titus 1:7; and 1 Peter 2:25 along with two places where the office is named instead of the person. See Acts 1:20 and 1 Timothy 3:1.). It seems that the *episcopos* was a person who carried out a function, that of overseeing the local congregation. It is possible that this term is analogous to the present clerk of the session, chairman of the board of deacons or official board, or the equivalent. It may be that this was not an office or even a function of the religious aspects of the congregation but rather oversight of the practical matters. It probably came to denote the local minister in charge, and later the one in charge of an area of the church.

Another term found frequently is *diakonos,* from which we get the word "deacon." The word means "servant" and may well have been used rather freely to designate anyone who used his or her talents in the ongoing work of the church. By later New Testament times, however, it seems to have evolved into a semi-official office of some sort (see 1 Timothy 3:8ff.). It is interesting to note that in Paul's time women could be designated as "deaconesses" (see Romans 16:1), and it is possible (though debated) that the passage found in 1 Timothy 3:11 refers to women who could also qualify for the position of deacon.

The picture which can be drawn from the New Testament itself about the structure of the church is sketchy indeed. One sees that early in the church's existence the "Twelve" exercised most authority. After this there was a larger group known as apostles, though it is not at all clear exactly what the requirements were to be named in this group. After this there seems to have been simply a large and diverse number of people who basically contributed to the church as the individuals had talent and the church had need. Some needs were more pressing and more uniform than others. There was always the need for teachers to instruct the new converts. There was always a need for someone to handle the material needs of the community, and so on. And finally, some type of "official" oversight of the group was necessary; this could be done by a group of people or only one person. And probably the movement was from the group to a single individual who was "first among equals."

It was not until late in the first century A.D., however, that there began to emerge a type of structure with "offices" to be filled in the church itself. This development is reflected in the New Testament by the Pastoral Epistles (First and Second Timothy and Titus). Later documents which were not included in the New Testament canon (the list of authoritative books) demonstrate this development as well (see, for example, the *Didache,* the *Letters of Ignatius of Antioch,* to name only a few). The main interest to the student of the New Testament and the church of today, however, is not so much what formal structure was present in the early church, but rather what the New Testament writers understood the nature of the church to be. This was much more important for them than the discussion over what external form the church should have, or whether the entire church should reflect the same beliefs, organization, and philosophy of clergy and sacrament.

When one approaches the New Testament writings, one finds that there are at least three characteristics of the early church reflected in the New Testament literature, especially in the letters of Colossians and Ephesians. These are all subordinate, however, to the belief that the church was the body of Christ, and that Christ was the head of the church. The early church was absolutely clear at this point: no Christ—no church. So any church today that attempts to be a church apart from the lordship over it of God's Messiah cannot be the church in the New Testament sense.

Because of the lordship of Christ the church then could be described by three characteristics: proclamation, witness, and love. First of all, the earliest church as reflected in the book of Acts was a church dedicated to the proclamation of the Good News (i.e., the gospel) about Jesus Christ. They felt that they had a message to proclaim, and proclaim it they did. We have already discussed briefly the content of the proclamation, the *kerygma* (see pp. 13-15).

But the church did not believe simply in words. Today many think that witnessing is done and over when one speaks the proper words. We live in an era of history when we are inundated with an ocean of words. Through words we communicate, and therefore we learn. Words are exceedingly important. That understanding was certainly present in the early church community as well, but to the early Christians words were not nearly enough. The transforming power of the Spirit, which was the sign that Jesus was indeed still alive and present with them, led in their experience inevitably to a new and different life-style characterized by the elements of a life completely different from the ways of the world.

In other words, the witnessing of the community was always a witness of the lives of the Christians demonstrating that something new was now available to the world. They also believed that this new life could unleash the Spirit of God so that the old ways would be destroyed, and that all human beings, and even the realm of nature, would be renewed. Their work, as the work of Christ, was to be a reconciling ministry in the universe. This kind of witness led to what one normally calls "good works." They did not believe that "good works" preceded or brought the new life, but rather they understood the "good works" to flow naturally out of the new life.

And these good works accomplished by Christian people were to be characterized by something new as well. People have throughout the ages done "good works" for a variety of reasons: to attempt to win the favor of the gods, or other people, or simply to salve guilty consciences—all triggered by less than the highest motives. The Christian belief was that these good works were to be done for and with a higher motivation. This motivation was love for God and for one's fellow human beings. In fact there is a good deal of evidence in the New Testament that "good deeds" done for anything other than the proper motives are worthless. The teaching of Jesus in the Sermon on the Mount reflects this emphasis. "On that day many will say to me, 'Lord, Lord, did we not prophesy in your name, and cast out demons in your name, and do many mighty works in your name?' And then will I declare to them, 'I never knew you; depart from me, you evildoers'" (Matthew 7:22-23).

This same teaching is reflected just as emphatically in Paul's teaching. When the people in Corinth were arguing about whose gift (talent) and contribution to the church were the greatest, Paul responded with his famous "hymn to love" in 1 Corinthians 13. The first few verses are worthy of mentioning here.

"If I speak with the tongues of men and of angels, but have not love, I am a noisy gong or a clanging cymbal. And if I have prophetic powers, and understand all mysteries and all knowledge, and if I have all faith, so as to remove mountains, but have not love, I am nothing. If I give away all I have, and if I deliver my body to be burned [Greek reading "in order that I may boast"], but have not love, I gain nothing" (1 Corinthians 13:1-3).

There was the clear recognition among the writers of the New Testament that there is a real difference in deeds done for the right reason and motivation and deeds done for the wrong reasons and motivation. Only the former can be truly "Christian," and these types of deeds are supposed to be characteristic of the people of the church.

If the people of the church could exemplify in their lives the characteristics which the New Testament writers saw as central to the life of the church, there the church can and will take root and grow. The problems of organization and structure and government are secondary problems. They do not make the church the church. Allegiance to the Head of the church, God's appointed Messiah, by a proclaiming, witnessing, and loving community of people brings unity to the church. It is not uniformity that the New Testament writers are concerned with, but real unity which comes through common commitment to a common Lord.

3 The Eschatology of the Early Church

The term "eschatology" means literally "a study of the end (or last things)." Most persons when they hear about "the end" naturally think in terms of the end of the world, the final wrap-up of all human history. This definition, however, is only one of the possibilities of understanding for the term in its biblical background. This broader spectrum of meaning results from the fact that not all "ends" are necessarily the end of the world. The word "eschatology" then has come to have various meanings. It can denote the end of all things; or it can denote the end of a period of time (an "age," for example); or it can also carry the idea of a significant event which can change the direction of one's life, or history, etc. Here the event is not the "last" in a series, but rather the determining event for later times. Thus, when one reads about "eschatology" in the New Testament writings, it is well to ask just what meaning is intended in that particular context, for the New Testament church understood eschatology with all these various nuances.

Interpreters of the New Testament have had some very heated exchanges in their attempts to understand the eschatological teachings of these writings. To put things in proper perspective, it is well for us to recall that the eschatology of the early church was centered in (though not exclusively confined to) the belief that Jesus would return soon to consummate the kingdom of God. Whether the disciples of Jesus had understood his teachings at this point correctly is a matter of debate, but that is not pertinent for our discussion. It is clear that the *kerygma* of the church, which was handed on to Paul, taught that Jesus would return soon. All other ideas and understandings of their faith were conditioned, at least to some degree, by this teaching. One very glaring example of how this idea could influence the life of the Christian can be seen clearly in 1 Corinthians 7.

In Corinth there had been a discussion about whether sexual activity, even within marriage, should be allowed. Some people obviously had been influenced by the Greek idea that the flesh was evil and sinful; and since sexual activity was connected quite clearly to the body, their understanding was that sexual activity was forbidden to a Christian. The people in Corinth wrote to Paul asking his advice and seeking his understanding in this matter. Paul tells them clearly and plainly that sexual activity within the marriage bond is not sinful in any way.

There is an added factor, however, that they should take into account. Paul reminds them that the Parousia is very near. It was the belief at that time that when the Parousia did occur, it would be preceded by a time of intense evil and persecution of the people of God by the forces of evil. Sexual activity (since pills, etc., were unknown in those days) would bring into the world small children, increase one's duties and responsibilities, and generally make life much more complicated in a time when the best possible situation would be where there were as few responsibilities and duties (humanly speaking) as one could have. Paul, therefore, counsels against marriage, not because there was anything wrong or inferior in that state (see 1 Corinthians 7:3-4, 28, 36-38), but because of the practical considerations which should be taken into account.

One can see, therefore, that this idea of an early return of Jesus did influence and affect many of the church's beliefs and actions. It is probably the main reason why there was no real structure or organization in the early church, and it caused other problems as well. Some people simply quit their jobs to wait for the Parousia (see 2 Thessalonians 3:6ff.), and there was little if any attempt made to prepare the church for the future (see Acts 4:32ff.).

The fact that the Parousia did not occur as expected created some problems, and in the latter part of the first century A.D. the church had to deal with the embarrassment caused by the Parousia's failure to materialize. Even within the lifetime of Paul one can detect a shift in Paul's eschatological thought. Some scholars have argued that Paul completely gave up his belief in the Parousia by the latter part of his life, but on close examination of Paul's writings one is hard pressed to find such a complete change in his thinking. It is obvious, however, that Paul did shift his emphasis somewhat.

In Paul's earliest writings (see First and Second Thessalonians) it is obvious that Paul expected the Parousia very shortly. One of the problems he faced with the Christians in Thessalonica arose from the fact that some of their loved ones had died. This raised the question as to whether those who had died would miss out on the joys of that great event. Paul assured the people who were concerned about their loved ones that those who had died would not in any way miss out on that great occasion. Somewhat later when Paul wrote to the Corinthians, it seems that he still believed that the Parousia would come within that generation. "We shall not all die [i.e., before the Parousia], but we shall all be changed" (1 Corinthians 15:51, author's paraphrase).

It is difficult to determine exactly what happened; but by the time Paul wrote Second Corinthians, there had been a definite shift in his thinking. Not that he had given up the idea of the Parousia, but he seems definitely to have shifted his emphasis to what happens to a Christian at and after death. In 2 Corinthians 4:16–5:5 he talks about "a house not made with hands, eternal in the heavens." And in Philippians (a letter probably written from Ephesus about the same time as Second Corinthians, approximately A.D. 55) he speaks about departing and being "with Christ, for that is far better" (Philippians 1:21-23). Some scholars have speculated that a serious danger to Paul's life during this period of his ministry may well have caused him to begin thinking that he himself might well die before the Parousia. And something like that may have been the cause of this shift in emphasis. The idea of the Parousia was not abandoned by Paul, however, for even in his last writings he referred to such an event (see Colossians 3:4).

But the Parousia did not come. The apostles were dying; Paul had died, and the entire first generation of Christians was disappearing very rapidly. Many had also believed that when Jerusalem would be captured by the Romans and the temple destroyed, this would signal the events of the "end." That event took place (A.D. 70), but still no Parousia. Therefore, after A.D. 70 (which is usually called the post-apostolic period) several different approaches seem to have been taken by the New Testament writers (which would reflect the thinking of the church during that time). First of all, especially early in that period, there were some who still believed that the Parousia was near. The writer of First Peter, writing probably soon after the destruction of the temple in A.D. 70, strongly believed that the end was still near.[1]

[1] For a fuller discussion of the dating and historical circumstances connected with the writings during this period, see James M. Efird, *The New Testament Writings: History, Literature, Interpretation* (Atlanta: John Knox Press, 1979), chapter 6.

But as the years progressed, other views came to be held, and these can be detected in the various New Testament writings from this period. Some seem simply to ignore the issue! The author of Ephesians speaks about the church in the "generations to come" (Ephesians 2:7) and outlines a long-range plan of attack and defense for the Christian against the world (see Ephesians 6:10ff.). There is in Ephesians no real reference to a Parousia. Other writers tend to reinterpret the meanings of "soon." The author of Second Peter probably gives the classic example of this type of explanation (an explanation which is, interestingly enough, used quite often even today!). He argues that "soon" to God is not to be confused with the human meaning of the term. ". . . with the Lord one day is as a thousand years, and a thousand years as one day" (2 Peter 3:8).

Even the book of Revelation, long held to be *the key* to the understanding of God's timetable for the end of the world, does not really teach the coming of the Parousia with the same understanding as Paul and the early church held.[2] But the most significant change seems to be reflected in the Gospel of John. Here one finds a major reinterpretation of what the "coming" of Jesus is supposed to be. Almost all of the future references have been done away with in this writing, and those which are left seem to mean something quite different from the earlier ideas. The emphasis in John's Gospel centers in a present transformation which gives *eternal life* (i.e., new life) to the Christian believer in the *present*. Because of this the future aspect of the Christian's life is oriented toward the time of the believer's death. "And when I go and prepare a place for you, I will come again and will take you to myself, that where I am you may be also" (John 14:3).

The author of the Fourth Gospel as well as some of the other New Testament writers had learned that "eschatology" did not have to do primarily with the "end" of all things. This preoccupation with the end of all history placed the emphasis upon a *quantity* of time, but later New Testament writers came to understand that the element of *quality* was much more important. The decisions that one makes do not necessarily indicate that at a certain point one is assured of safety somewhere in the future. But rather the decisions one makes relate to quality of life. This life is not ordinary life as commonly known, but it is a new quality of existence which gives meaning and purpose and direction to one's being so that life has focus and a goal to pursue. But

[2] For the teaching of Revelation, see James M. Efird, *Daniel and Revelation: A Study of Two Extraordinary Visions* (Valley Forge: Judson Press, 1978).

to understand eschatology in this way is not to deny the validity of the future aspects by any means!

There is definitely in New Testament teaching a real and direct connection between what one is now, in this life, and what one will be later on. The decisions made in the present affect the future. This is why one cannot really separate the two into neat categories. The future impinges upon the present, and present decisions mark the direction of the future. The Christian writers knew this clearly, even if some of them were mistaken about the nature and time of the Parousia.

Having studied the New Testament for some years now, I have come to the conclusion that there would be less confusion about eschatology if the eschatology of the New Testament could be viewed as a "teleology." Teleology has to do with a purpose, a goal to be accomplished, a battle to be won, a life that is brought to completion or maturity. This emphasizes both the present and future aspects of the call God makes to the Christian. Too many people when thinking about eschatology have emphasized only the aspects about the "end," but in the biblical accounts the emphasis is in reality upon a new beginning. Those who are so preoccupied with the end of the world would be better served and closer to New Testament thought overall to be concerned with the new life given by God which transforms the person, and the society of persons likewise committed, into a moving force within the world to accomplish God's purpose of reconciliation. This person in the new relationship fears nothing from death because the new relationship transcends death by giving new life. This new life is not affected by physical death because it belongs to a different order of existence, an order where God and his people can never be separated from each other.

Having given this all too brief overview of Christology, ecclesiology, and eschatology, let us turn to examine two specific New Testament writings, Colossians and Ephesians. It is quite appropriate to do so, for these three themes lie at the heart of these books and are explicated in a much deeper way. What has been said here in general about the Christ, the church, and the end should be kept in mind as one studies these two great documents so that their distinct and specific teaching can illuminate our understanding of these three important areas of Christian thought.

4

Background Considerations

When one turns to examine any one of the biblical writings, it is extremely helpful to the understanding of the message of the book to be as familiar as one can be with the circumstances which surrounded the time when the author wrote the work. Too often many persons fail to remember that the Bible as it has been written, preserved, and transmitted has a history that is often intriguing as well as fascinating. And each book has its own history, a set of historical circumstances which is unique to it.

This is especially true with the New Testament writings in general and the Pauline letters in particular. Far too often we have heard about Paul as the first Christian theologian, and many systems of theology have been based upon Paul's writings (especially on the Epistle to the Romans). But of all the New Testament literature, Paul's letters are the most "occasional," i.e., they were written at a particular time, in a particular place, to a particular group of people, for a particular purpose, often to combat specific problems that had arisen in the church.

That Paul was a letter writer is an established fact. In reality he wrote many letters that have simply been lost (see 1 Corinthians 5:9; 2 Corinthians 2:4; etc.). Each of his letters was sent to a church or, in a few instances, to a group of churches. These letters were obviously cherished for a while, but then seem to have lost their appeal and authority. This may be the reason that some of them were lost. In the latter part of the first century, however, someone collected the letters of Paul (or at least as many as could be recovered) into a body or "corpus." It appears that this collection had been made before the early part of the second century A.D., because certain church figures in that period seem to have known of the collection and had access to the letters in a single place. These were the first of the New Testament writings to have been collected, but it was not long thereafter that the Four Gospels were gathered together. Later the other writings were also collected, and gradually these three basic collections were accepted as authoritative by the leadership of the Christian church (i.e., by the end of the fourth century A.D.).

When one reads the letters of the great apostle Paul, one is immediately confronted with problems related to the proper understanding and interpretation of his writings. This became evident very early, for the author of Second Peter (probably the last New Testament book to be written) says of Paul's letters: "So also our beloved Paul wrote to you according to the wisdom given him, speaking of this as he does in all his letters. There are some things in them hard to understand, which the ignorant and unstable twist to their own destruction, as they do the other scriptures" (2 Peter 3:15-16).

In all probability one of the chief problems involved in attempting to understand Paul's letters through the ages of church history is rooted in the fact that many have failed to understand and investigate the "occasion" which called for the writing of these particular words to those particular people. Too many want to read Paul's writings as if they were written by a theologian to other theologians rather than by a pastor to his congregation! Therefore, in order (we hope) to understand better the writings known to us as the Epistle to the Colossians and the Epistle to the Ephesians, we need to consider those questions which have to do with the background which called each into existence.

There is one further dimension with which the person who wishes to study the letters of Paul should be acquainted. Almost every good study of any of Paul's letters will assume certain ideas and questions about the writings which may sound strange to the uninformed reader. These questions stem from a certain approach to the study of the New Testament writings which occurred in the first half of the nineteenth century. Under the direction of a brilliant scholar named F. C. Baur at Tübingen (a university in Germany) a theory was propounded as to how and under what circumstances the New Testament writings originated. Part of that discussion naturally centered on the writings of Paul.

In this "system" it was thought that Paul wrote only four letters: Romans, Galatians, First and Second Corinthians, and these were designated as the *Haupbriefe* (chief or authentic letters). The others were thought to be from other persons at other moments in the history of the church. In present scholarship, however, much of the old "Tübingen" theory has been rejected. But two points from that school still seem to persist in Pauline studies: (1) the question about the "authenticity" of the letter (i.e., was it really written by Paul or by someone writing in Paul's name?), and (2) the question about the "unity" of the letter (i.e., is the letter as we have it a unity or does it appear to be a document that has supplemental fragments of other letters incorporated into it?). In other words, the two most persistent critical questions which are discussed by interpreters of Paul's letters are the questions dealing with "authenticity" and "unity." These two points, along with others, will be examined as we turn to look at the background material for Colossians and Ephesians.

Colossians

Traditionally speaking, both the letters of Colossians and Ephesians have been considered a part of what is usually designated "Paul's Prison Correspondence." These are the letters to the Colossians, Philemon, the Philippians, and the Ephesians. The date and place of that imprisonment have been understood as A.D. 60-62 in Rome (see Acts 28). There are, however, certain problems which one encounters in accepting that date and that place if one studies with some care the specific words of the writings. In some of the writing the historical time period seems to be closer to the middle of Paul's work in Ephesus (about A.D. 55) than it does to the Roman period. Further, reference to the gifts the people have sent to Paul, Paul's travel plans, and the intensity of the danger to Paul's person seem to reflect a place and a time other than Rome.

Two alternative places, and therefore dates as well, have been suggested as the origin for these letters. One possibility is Caesarea (see Acts 23:31–26:32). Paul was detained under guard there for two years before he finally appealed his case to be heard before Caesar. If this is the setting, the date would be about A.D. 58-60. Very few, however, argue for the Caesarean origin presently. Another conjecture has been Ephesus, sometime during the third journey. We know from Acts that Paul spent from two to three years there (approximately A.D. 54-57), and we know from his writings that he experienced numerous imprisonments (see 2 Corinthians 11:23) not specifically mentioned in Acts or Paul's own writings. This theory that the prison letters are from Ephesus answers many of the questions about time and place that are raised by a Roman origin for the letters. Many, however, are reluctant to accept an Ephesian origin because we know *specifically* of no Ephesian imprisonment either from Acts or Paul's letters. Paul says that he "fought with beasts at Ephesus" (see 1 Corinthians 15:32) and expresses thanks to Prisca and Aquila for their risking "their necks for my life" (see Romans 16:3-4). We know from Acts that these two were with Paul in Ephesus during his ministry there, but they were also at Corinth while Paul labored in that place as well. So the problem remains, and scholars are very dubious about establishing an Ephesian imprisonment without some specific evidence to support such a claim.

It is important to wrestle with such questions, however, for the decision one makes about the matter of origin may have some bearing upon the interpretation of certain passages. But, alas, certainty cannot be assured in every instance.

The letter to the Colossians claims to have been written by Paul while he was in prison (the location is not specifically stated) to the people in the church at Colossae. Paul did not found this church directly, but his lieutenant, Epaphras, established the church while Paul was in Ephesus during the third journey. Some problem had arisen in the church there dealing with "false teaching" or "philosophy and empty deceit" (see Colossians 2:8) which threatened to lead the saints astray in terms of their opinion of Jesus and in their daily living. Paul wrote to these people to counter this false teaching.

The problems involved with the origin of this letter have to do with (1) the authenticity of the letter, (2) the place and date of writing, and (3) the specific type and source of the "false teaching" being addressed. We shall examine each of these areas separately.

Since the time of the old Tübingen school the authenticity (i.e., the Pauline authorship) of Colossians has been questioned. To say this is not to raise doubts about its inspiration or authority as a canonical book of Scripture; but the question is raised as to whether Paul actually wrote this letter, or if he wrote it in the form in which it now exists. In that era of history, pseudonymity, i.e., writing in the name of someone else, was a common practice and did not carry with it the stigma that such an act would have today. Therefore, one should not be surprised to find writings in the Bible itself which were composed in this manner. Again, it must be emphasized that this practice does not detract in any way from the inspiration and authority of the writing. To understand that this practice was common in that time, was not considered "immoral," and could have been the method of writing used even by some biblical authors may very well be valuable thoughts to remember when approaching a biblical book. To examine each book carefully to ascertain as accurately as possible the historical background and circumstances of that writing cannot but make the message of the book clearer.

But why, specifically, do some scholars think that Paul did not write Colossians? There are several reasons. One finds in certain parts of Colossians a style of writing and the use of words which one does not find in most of the other Pauline letters acknowledged almost universally to have been written by Paul. Further, some argue that the heresy which is being combated in this letter seems to have come into existence only in the second century A.D., long after Paul's death. And finally, there are certain ideas contained in this short writing which one does not find in other Pauline works, such as Christ as the head of the church (the body), the rather exalted teaching about Jesus, the emphasis on marriage and its long-range implications, as well as others. Some scholars feel, therefore, that these factors all add up to the likelihood that someone else, writing later, wrote this letter in the name of Paul to speak to a church situation that needed some careful analysis and strong challenge. If indeed Paul did not write this letter, it could have been written at any time up to about A.D. 100 by an unknown author. Where it originated cannot be known either; a good guess would be in the area of Asia Minor around Ephesus.

More and more scholars of late, however, are concluding that there is not enough evidence to deny that Paul really did write this letter. The following arguments are the most frequently used. On examination it is quite clear that the change in vocabulary and style only occurs in those places where the author is discussing the main points of the "false teaching" present in the church. This would account for the new vocabulary, and the change in style as well. The remainder, which is the majority, of the letter does reflect the Pauline style and vocabulary. On this score, there appears to be no reason to deny the letter to Paul.

The argument about the nature and date of the "heresy" is more elusive. The false teachers in Colossae seem to have derived their basic teaching from a "gnostic" type thought pattern which had become widespread in the Greco-Roman world and had even influenced Jewish thought, especially in certain areas of the Roman Empire. The Colossae area was one such place where this had occurred. The full-scale gnostic systems did not develop finally until the second century A.D., thus causing some to argue that the type of false teaching at Colossae could not have been current during Paul's lifetime. But gnostic thought patterns were quite widespread in the first century A.D. and were encountered by Paul at Corinth. Therefore, this factor does not make a late date necessary for this letter.

But what exactly was *gnosticism?* It was a type of belief which was founded on the idea of a dualistic nature of the universe. God was good, pure, Spirit and as such could have no relationship with evil, impure matter. There was, therefore, between God and the created world a superstructure of other "beings" (sometimes called *archons,* principalities or powers) which descended toward the created order, held dominion and power over the created order because they (or one of their number closest to the world as we know it) had created it. A spark of the divine had somehow gotten into the creation of the human race, so that human beings (or their souls, a *non*biblical idea) longed for salvation, i.e., the release from bondage to these powers and from being imprisoned in the evil created order. Salvation, therefore, consisted in release from this world so that the "spirit" could be reunited with God.

This salvation could be accomplished by one's learning or acquiring the knowledge (Greek=*gnosos*) of how the "overworld" or "superstructure" was composed. This "overworld" was sometimes called the *pleroma,* or fullness. With the knowledge of how this group was put together, the soul could make its way back to God, be released from bondage to this world, and be reunited with God. All of this could be accomplished by means of "knowledge," thus the term "gnosticism."

The kind of thinking that was attached to this thought pattern usually led to two extremes. One included those people who felt that the world as we know it is so evil, corrupt, and horrible that the truly "spiritual" person should keep oneself away from as much of the world and have as little contact with the world as possible. Therefore, asceticism, usually in an extreme form, came to be one of the characteristics of such persons.

The second group consisted of the other extreme. These persons believed that since they were now "spiritual" and that the created world was basically evil, this world and its standards no longer had any claim on them. They could do anything they wanted to do anytime, anywhere, with anyone! The flesh does not count; the spirit does. Therefore, there were no rules in the material world which could be binding on them.

While it is true that the full-blown gnostic systems did not come into existence until the second century A.D., there is enough evidence from nonbiblical sources to support the claim that these *ideas* were nevertheless a part of the first century A.D. And it is a fact that this type of thinking was found by Paul in the church at Corinth. (The Corinthian letters, incidentally, are not denied to Paul!) If one carefully examines 1 Corinthians 5–7, one can see both of these extremes, asceticism and libertinism, causing trouble in the church there. And Corinthians was written about A.D. 55! Therefore, on this count, there is no need to postulate a late date for the writing of the Colossian letter.

The last set of arguments which casts doubt upon Pauline authorship of Colossians lies in the area of religious teaching and ideas. Some see the idea of Jesus as the head of the church rather than the idea of the church as the body of Christ (see 1 Corinthians 12) and the exalted concepts about Jesus as evidence of non-Pauline authorship. But these ideas are either not all that new and different or they occur in precisely those areas where the author is dealing with the philosophical teaching which he is attempting to combat. There is also the emphasis in this letter on the family and marriage which seems to be different from that found in 1 Corinthians 7. It is, however, possible to understand this as either an advancement of Paul's thinking or his speaking precisely to some problem in the Colossian church about which we have no indication except for his brief comment in Colossians 3:18ff. Therefore in this area also there really seems to be little evidence to cause us to doubt the traditional view that Paul is indeed the author of this letter.

One final note should be appended at this point. There is strong evidence that Colossians and the letter to Philemon have a common origin (compare Philemon vv. 23-24 with Colossians 4:10-17). And no one really argues that Paul did not write Philemon. It would seem, therefore, that this fact, coupled with the other arguments which we have just examined, makes it quite certain that Paul did write the letter to the Colossians.

Therefore, for the purpose of background understanding for our investigation of the teaching and meaning of Colossians, we shall assume that Paul wrote the letter to the Colossians, from a Roman imprisonment about A.D. 60-62, for the basic purpose of giving the Christians at Colossae instruction concerning false teaching which was threatening to confuse their thinking about matters pertaining to the place of Christ in relation to the world and to how that false teaching might change their understanding of the Christian life-style.

Ephesians

As has been indicated earlier, traditionally the epistle to the Ephesians was written by Paul from prison, probably at Rome, approximately A.D. 62. Again, as with Colossians, there are problems with this understanding, but considerably more so with Ephesians than with Colossians.

In the first place it is known from the earliest Greek manuscripts of this writing that it had no specific destination originally. The words *in Ephesus* (1:1) are not found in the earliest Greek manuscripts; they were later added to give a specific destination to the letter. There are no personal greetings in this letter and the writing addresses no specific localized problem, at least none that is evident upon reading the document. Some have conjectured, therefore, that the letter (even if by Paul) was originally a circular letter intended to be read in various churches in a given area. Others have even conjectured that a space was deliberately left in the original manuscript so that the name of the church where it was being read could be inserted. This is possible but not probable. Adding to the mystery at this point is the fact that Marcion (an early second-century heretic but an admirer of Paul) knew this letter but called it the letter to the Laodiceans. This letter "from Laodicea" is mentioned in Colossians 4:16, and it is probably lost (even though a few think that the letter to Philemon may be that letter).

Nevertheless, Ephesians has been known from the earliest records as part of the Pauline body of letters even though it has not always been designated as "To the Ephesians."

Many of the same arguments made which cast doubt upon the Pauline authorship of Colossians are applicable also for Ephesians. There is the argument concerning the different vocabulary and style, the different religious ideas, and the different time-setting. In addition to these there is also the problem of how to evaluate the noticeable fact that Ephesians is quite dependent on Colossians. If one compares the two writings closely (especially in the original Greek), one finds that over one-third of Colossians is reproduced in Ephesians. Strangely enough, however, with only one or two exceptions the words are scattered in various passages as if being quoted from memory, but the memory is not quite perfect! And there is the curious fact in addition that the same words are used but often with different meaning!

Coupled with this is the strange phenomenon that one finds in Ephesians allusions to Paul's other writings sometimes even to the point of practically seeing Paul quote himself! If one carefully studies this situation, one finds phrases which recall parts of all of Paul's other letters, with the exception of Second Thessalonians, the most notable being echoes from Romans (Romans 3:21–4:2 in Ephesians 2:4-9), First Corinthians (1 Corinthians 3:9-16 in Ephesians 2:19-22 and 1 Corinthians 15:24-28 in Ephesians 1:20-23), and—of all things—Philemon (Philemon 1 in Ephesians 3:1 and Philemon 5 in Ephesians 1:15). There are others, but these will suffice to demonstrate the point.[1]

The question as to why Paul would "quote" himself to such an extent as is done in Ephesians is difficult to answer. There are many possible solutions but very few probable ones. The answer which seems to make the most sense is one that sees in Ephesians an attempt on the part of an ardent admirer of Paul to summarize the essential elements of Pauline thought for another day and another time. Some have speculated that the treatise was written as a summary of Paul's thought to be used as an introduction for the collection of Paul's letters. But the problem here is that we have never found that letter standing first in the collection, if it was indeed the introduction to it. In some way it seems to be related to the collection, but exactly how remains a mystery.

As for the vocabulary and style of this letter being different from Paul's usual letters, consider these items. There are over ninety words used in Ephesians which are not found in any of the writings generally accepted to be from Paul. The style of Paul's writing consists usually of shorter sentences which are to the point. The style of Ephesians consists of long and flowing sentences which sometimes seem to go on forever! This has been hidden from the English readers by the majority of the translations, because they have made shorter sentences complete with finite verbs of the longer sentences in the Greek which are filled with participles and phrases which flow from one to the other in unending order. For examples of this read the following as if each passage were one sentence in English (because they are in Greek): 1:3-14; 1:15-23; 2:1-10; 3:1-9. It is interesting to consider the fact that the average length of a sentence in Ephesians is almost twice the length of the average sentence in Paul's other letters!

As if this were not enough to contemplate, there is also the consideration that many terms used by Paul in other letters (notably

[1] For a detailed and brilliant discussion of these technical matters, see C. Leslie Mitton, *The Epistle to the Ephesians: Its Authorship, Origin and Purpose* (Oxford: The Clarendon Press, 1951).

Colossians) are used differently in Ephesians. For example, the term "church" is almost always used of a specific congregation in Paul's letters; in Ephesians it always means the one universal church, the sum total of all the congregations. The word "mystery," as used in Colossians, seems to indicate the act of God in Christ for redemption, but in Ephesians it seems to mean the universe being joined together in Christ. The Greek word *oikonomia* is used in Colossians with the sense of "task" or "duty to perform," but in Ephesians it seems to mean "plan" or "purpose" of God!

The examples could be multiplied, but these will suffice to demonstrate the problems. It is not that Paul himself could not use words or terms with different meanings in different places, but the question remains as to why he would use so many terms so differently in this one letter. Couple this with the other considerations of vocabulary, style, as well as certain theological differences, and one is left in great bewilderment as to who the author of Ephesians might be.

As indicated, there are certain changes in the religious teachings of Ephesians from Paul's other letters. A few illustrations will be sufficient for our purposes here to demonstrate the point.

First, one is struck in Paul's letters by the importance of the cross and by what God accomplished through the cross, i.e., reconciliation of the world to himself. This can be seen in almost any of the genuine Pauline letters, but one sees this clearly in 2 Corinthians 5:16-21; Romans 5:1-11; even Colossians 1:19-20. But in Ephesians the cross, even though present, does not hold a prominent place at all, the emphasis centering upon the exaltation of Christ. And the reconciliation which is done on behalf of the human race is accomplished not by God working through Christ but by Christ himself! ". . . that [Jesus] might create in himself one new man in place of the two, so making peace, and might reconcile us both to God in one body through the cross, thereby bringing the hostility to an end" (Ephesians 2:15-16).

Secondly, when one reads Paul's letters carefully, one finds a strong belief in the imminence of the Parousia, i.e., the nearness of Jesus' return. In fact some of his teaching was based upon his belief that Jesus would return within the people's own lifetimes (See 1 Corinthians 7 where Paul counsels the people not to marry, not because marriage is wrong, but because the Parousia is so near!). Even in the letter to the Colossians one finds an emphasis on this very item (see Colossians 3:4). In Ephesians, however, one finds no reference to an early return but rather a challenge to the church to remain faithful for generations to come! ". . . that in the coming ages he might show the immeasurable riches of his grace toward us in Christ Jesus" (2:7). ". . . to him be glory in the church and in Christ Jesus to all generations, for ever and ever" (3:21). And the brilliant description of the armor available to a Christian to combat the evils of life (see 6:10-20) seems to assume a long and hard battle for the church and its members through the coming generations of human history. There is certainly a different "flavor" to the eschatological teachings of Ephesians when compared to the accepted Pauline writings.

In Ephesians 2:10 the reader finds the expression "good works." When one meditates on that for a moment, the thought immediately strikes home: Would Paul have ever used such a phrase? It was not that Paul was opposed to "good works," but during his ministry one of the most difficult problems he had to face was the idea that salvation could be obtained by "good works." Whether "good works" meant doing good deeds or keeping the ceremonial rituals of the old Jewish law is irrelevant. Paul avoided using this kind of term quite consciously. It is not impossible that he could have used it, but the question remains as to whether it is likely that he would have.

Finally, there is the question as to whether the evidence of the text itself supports the historical period of time known in the ministry of Paul or whether there is evidence pointing to another moment of history. And the text of Ephesians does give some clear indications at this point. During Paul's lifetime the great controversy was over whether Gentiles could become a part of the Christian movement, and, assuming that they could, what kind of obligation was to be incumbent upon them in regard to keeping the old Jewish laws. There was, in short, during Paul's lifetime a real tension between Jew and Gentile. As the church continued to grow, and since the Jewish-Roman war of A.D. 66-70 had in effect destroyed the old "home base" of the church in Jerusalem, this tension between Jew and Gentile in the church diminished. To a great degree the church as it developed became more and more Gentile in nature.

In Paul's letters we find this tension between Jew and Gentile in the church occupying the thought and energy of the great apostle quite frequently. He always appealed for unity between the two and even argued that these distinctions have been done away in Christ (see Galatians 3:28; Romans 10:12; Colossians 3:11). In the letter to the Ephesians, however, this tension and controversy seem to be a thing of the past. In fact, the great problem is that the church, which seems now to be predominantly Gentile, may be in danger of forgetting its historical roots in Judaism. And there is an air of thanksgiving about the fact that now Jews and Gentiles are one together in the church. No real tension is indicated.

Another point which directs one's attention to a time other than that of Paul is the fact that this author looks back to the foundation of the church as based on the "apostles and the prophets" (2:20). Paul always insists that the church has only one foundation and that is Christ himself (see 1 Corinthians 3:11). In Ephesians Jesus has become the "chief cornerstone." Further, in 3:5 there is a reference to "the holy apostles." Paul uses the word "holy" as a designation for each Christian, as one "set apart" for God and Christ. Here the term seems to indicate persons who have attained a superior status because of the quality of their lives or by virtue of their work in the church. This is quite un-Pauline.

The issues and points of similarity and difference between Paul's letters and Ephesians have been argued for many years, and the interpreters are genuinely divided about the Pauline authorship of Ephesians. The evidence is considered weighty on one side, and then on the other. But there is yet one additional problem. If Paul did not write the letter, then who did? And why? This set of questions has plagued those who argued for the non-Pauline origin. There has been one rather full theory set forth to explain these questions with which almost every interpreter of the epistle to the Ephesians must deal. This is the theory originally set forth by E. J. Goodspeed, which he later amplified along with one of his more noted students, John Knox.[2]

The theory goes something like this. After Paul's death in Rome, about A.D. 65, Paul was basically forgotten. But with the publication of Luke's work, Luke-Acts, there was a renewed interest in this great apostle and his work. Someone who was very familiar with the letter to the Colossians and who was a great admirer of Paul used this time to collect together the letters of Paul, or at least all that could be found. Having done that, this faithful admirer proceeded to write a letter of introduction to Paul's thought using the epistle which he knew best, Colossians, as the basis, but drawing upon the other letters as well. This would explain the fact that originally the letter had no

---

[2] See E. J. Goodspeed, *The Meaning of Ephesians* (Chicago: University of Chicago Press, 1933), and John Knox, *Philemon Among the Letters of Paul.* Rev. ed. (Nashville: Abingdon Press, 1959). Original edition, 1935.

specific reference to a particular church and why there are almost no references in the letter to specific problems or persons known to Paul. The only exception is at the end of the letter where the personal notation from Colossians is copied into the text of Ephesians!

The question which immediately follows this consideration naturally is: Who would have done this? We know from a series of letters written by one Ignatius of Antioch (who was on his way to Rome to be martyred) something about the church at Ephesus about A.D. 110–115. One of Ignatius's letters was sent to that church. In this letter he urged the people to honor their bishop, whose name was Onesimus. It is most interesting that the name of the slave on whose behalf Paul wrote to Philemon (a letter sent at the same time and to the same place as Colossians) was Onesimus. It was the speculation, therefore, that the bishop at Ephesus was none other than the same Onesimus who at one time had belonged to Philemon! Who would have owed any more to Paul than Onesimus? And he would have had access to Colossians and, of course, Philemon—the two letters most utilized (percentage wise at least) in the letter to the Ephesians.

The argument then was that Onesimus collected the letters of Paul together at Ephesus, wrote Ephesians in honor and memory of his benefactor to introduce Pauline thought to the churches of his area, thus explaining why Ephesians became a part of the Pauline corpus and also why it came to be known as the Epistle to the Ephesians. The letter originated there and was probably closely linked to that place in the minds of the early church. The date of all this most probably was somewhere around A.D. 90.

Not everyone accepts every part of Goodspeed's theory, not even those who feel that it is basically correct. But the point is that such a theory as this does give a specific context for the writing of Ephesians if Paul is not its author.

Summary

To the average reader and Bible student all the discussions about these historical and technical matters may seem bewildering and unnecessary. Yet the fact is that the books of our Bible do have a *Sitz im Leben,* a "setting in life," and if we can ascertain what setting that was, we shall be in a better position to understand and to interpret the sacred writings. The task of the twentieth-century biblical interpreter is quite frustrating at points, because the recovery of the historical setting of the books is sometimes very difficult and tedious. It is necessary, however, so that the religious truth contained within these writings can be clearly seen and understood and so that the truth will not be confused with the container in which it is held.

It will perhaps best serve our purposes to give a brief summary of what has been discussed so that the stage may be clearly set for the exposition of the two letters under consideration here.

Even though some scholars have questioned the Pauline authorship of Colossians, the conclusion reached here is that there is no good reason to deny that the letter is genuinely from Paul. Further, there is no good reason to question the tradition that the letter originated from Rome, about A.D. 60-62. The purpose of the writing was to warn the church at Colossae about certain "false teaching" which was questioning the place of Christ in the order of creation and redemption and also advocating certain "life-styles" which related to this particular type of thought but which Paul saw as a threat to the truly Christian life.

The letter to the Ephesians, however, is another matter. Most think that Ephesians is a circular letter or a general treatise (whether by Paul or not), because the evidence points to the fact that the superscription "To the Ephesians" was a later designation of the letter. The question of authorship is a very sticky problem with this writing, however. If one accepts the tradition, the letter would be accepted as by Paul, from a Roman prison, about A.D. 62. But we have examined some of the weighty evidence which points in the direction of someone other than Paul and to a time period later than Paul. This is the assumption, therefore, which will be followed in the exposition of Ephesians here, namely, that the author was an ardent admirer of Paul, who wrote this magnificent epistle as an attempt to utilize Paul's own teaching (and in several instances, his own words) to speak to a church situation in his own time, approximately A.D. 90. To understand the origin of the writing in this way in no way detracts from its inspiration or authority. It merely helps us to understand the teaching more clearly.

5 Colossians— An Exposition

The city of Colossae was located in ancient Phrygia in the Lycus River valley (in the western part of present-day Turkey) and was important in that it was on the trade route to and from Ephesus. Earlier in its history it appears to have been a great and populous city according to some of the ancient historians, but by the New Testament period it had begun to lose some of its importance. Two neighboring cities, Hierapolis and Laodicea, had increased in size and importance at the expense of Colossae. The city did exist for some time after this, but ultimately became deserted. It is still deserted today, and, surprisingly enough, little or no archaeological research has been done there!

What kind of people comprised the ethnic makeup of this place? In all probability there was a mixture of native Phrygians along with Greeks and Jews. The Jews had been settled in that area in the second century B.C. by the Seleucid king, Antiochus III. As one can imagine, the cultural and religious milieu was a mixed one with all sorts of Phrygian, Greek, and Jewish elements part of the total picture.

The church there had been founded, in all probability, during the time when Paul was at Ephesus (about A.D. 54-57). This evangelizing work was obviously done by one of Paul's able converts named Epaphras (see 1:7; 4:12-13), who at the time of the writing of the letter to the Colossians was sharing with Paul his imprisonment, whether voluntarily or involuntarily we do not know. Paul himself, therefore, was not personally acquainted with the church as a whole but probably did know some of the individual members. Most of the people in the church at Colossae were Gentiles (see 1:21, 27; 2:13) even though some interpreters argue for a more active Jewish contingency.

The occasion for the writing of the letter arose from some "false teaching" which apparently was threatening to lead those new Christians astray in three ways. First, there was the problem of identifying Christ with other beings in the created order, thus denying to him the unique place in God's redeeming and reconciling process. Secondly, there was the real danger of the church's slipping into a "gnostic" type of understanding, i.e., believing that salvation could come through certain knowledge which the "learned and wise" possessed. And finally, there was the problem of how this "false doctrine" could and was leading to a life-style that was out of line with the new life in Christ as understood and preached by Paul and the other early Christian leaders. It is an interesting point to note when studying the New Testament writings that "exactly correct" beliefs are usually viewed more loosely than proper life-style. False teaching was viewed as especially dangerous when it led to improper living! Paul's response to the Colossian church reflects this concern.

There is yet one further matter which should be mentioned before turning to the text of Colossians. In that period of history there was a definite pattern in letter writing which can be briefly outlined and will assist in interpreting Paul's letters. First there was a salutation in which the writer identified himself and gave greetings to the person(s) to whom the letter was addressed. This was followed by a thanksgiving, usually to the god or gods for various and sundry kindnesses. These reasons for thanksgiving usually related to the people with whom the letter was concerned. After this there followed the main body of the letter outlining the purpose and concerns involved for the writing. This was followed by some concluding remarks.

Paul's letters generally follow this same outline. The only real difference seems to be in the main body of the letter where some interpreters find a two-fold breakdown. The problem(s) which he is addressing is discussed usually "theoretically" (or some say "theologically"), and this is completed by an "ethical" section which exhorts the people to live godly and Christlike lives. The technical term for such ethical exhortation is *paraenesis (parenesis)*. Not all of Paul's letters yield themselves to such a neat division (see Romans 1–11; 12–15, for example), however, because Paul in his own mind probably did not neatly divide his Christian ideology between "theology" on the one hand and "ethics" on the other. Quite often his theology and ethics are twined together in such a way that they are simply inseparable. But it is good to keep in mind when studying any of Paul's letters that in many cases the body of the letter will fall into two distinct (but not separate) divisions.

Because of the limitations of space the biblical text of Colossians (and later Ephesians) will not be reproduced here, but the reader is urged to read each biblical passage before looking at the expository and exegetical comments in this book. This method will give a much deeper appreciation and understanding of what the great apostle was attempting to say to those people who lived over nineteen hundred years ago—and will assist us in understanding what he is saying to our society in the present.

Colossians 1:1-2: Here one sees the usual epistolary salutation as it was utilized in those days. Paul identifies himself and even calls himself "an apostle of Christ Jesus." This is his usual self-designation, but it is exceedingly appropriate in this letter, because Paul is not known to these people personally nor did he directly establish their church. The title "apostle" in the New Testament seems to have had several different meanings, but in each instance it was a title that carried with it a high degree of authority and respect. Timothy, Paul's trusted young assistant, is also with Paul and is named in the salutation with him as one who also sends greetings and, in all probability, concurs with Paul in what he is about to say.

The letter is addressed to the "saints" in Colossae. The term "saint" is used by Paul to designate the people of God. The word *hagios* is a translation into Greek of the Old Testament Hebrew word for "holy," which had as its basic meaning the idea of being "set apart," "other than." Christians are those who have been "set apart" by God for a particular purpose. This understanding of the "saints" is quite similar to the Old Testament idea of the Israel of God, a people called out to be the instrument of God's revelation in the world. The best translation here would probably be, "to the saints in Colossae, even (or also) faithful brothers and sisters in Christ."

The usually accepted Greek greeting in those days was the infinitive form of the Greek word *chairō*, to rejoice, be glad, which came to mean "welcome," "a cheery hello," "greetings." Paul uses a word from the same family, but he utilizes the noun *charis*, which means grace, favor, or gracious care which indicates something of his own understanding of the Christian faith as a free gift of God. He couples this with the old Jewish greeting, *shalom*, peace. Peace in the Old Testament (and New Testament) setting means something quite broader than simply a cessation of hostility, a truce, or a time when nothing negative is happening. *Shalom* designates the totality of all the good things that God can give in this world; a good translation might be something like "total well-being." So when Paul greets the saints of the churches with "grace and peace," he is in reality giving to them a special blessing at the very beginning of his letter!

Colossians 1:3-8: Paul now enters into the thanksgiving section. He indicates that he has heard of their faith in Christ Jesus and the love which they have for each other. Perhaps it would be wise at this point to discuss briefly the idea of "faith" as it is used in Paul's letters. As with any writer, certain words can be used with more than one meaning—and Paul is no exception. There are, however, certain meanings that tend to be predominant for certain words. The word "faith" does not for Paul indicate a set of theological doctrines which one believes and is therefore "saved." This idea is nothing more or less than a form of gnosticism (salvation by knowledge) which Paul struggled against throughout his ministry. Faith is, in Paul's writings, primarily a commitment of one's life to God in Christ in trusting obedience. It is not something that one can earn; neither is it something that anyone deserves. God has freely offered a "way out" for the human race from the morass of sin and evil in which it is submerged and from which it cannot extricate itself. Human beings must accept the free gift of God, committing their lives to God in Christ and entrusting themselves in total obedience to him. This is basically what faith is: it is a positive, trusting, obedient, and total acceptance of God and all that God has done for the world in and through the person of Jesus, the Messiah of God.

This faith commitment opens the lives of persons to be receptive to the transforming Spirit of God which works in and through people to make of them something which they cannot be by themselves. This is why Paul links directly within this thanksgiving the idea of faith in Christ with the idea of "love for the saints."

At this point (v. 5) Paul introduces the idea of "hope laid up for you in heaven." This use of hope is not unusual for Paul, because he argues in most of his letters that hope is to be one of the distinguishing features of the Christian (see Romans 5:1ff.; 8:24ff.; 1 Corinthians 13:13, for example). This hope is naturally for the future, but it seems to be a hope that is both for this world as well as beyond or above this world. It is quite possible that Paul very early in this letter is already laying the groundwork for his debate with the "false teaching," which probably emphasized the future hope which the "false teachers" promised could only come later because of "knowledge." Paul likes to emphasize that the Christian's life begins *now, in the present, in this world*. It is quite possible that the "false teachers" were arguing that the present world matters not; that it is only the future that counts; and Christianity is too concerned with the present. Paul emphasizes that this is untrue by his comment that the Christian's hope is already "laid up in heaven" but is the culmination of a long process. Christianity emphasizes both the present and the future, neither to the detriment of the other.

The emphasis is upon the fact that the Christian gospel is *truth*, i.e., real and authentic, genuine, not of human origin, and that it is growing in the world, a sure sign that others also find truth in it. Paul uses this opportunity to say that Epaphras was with him and that his information came from that one who was dear to them and to whom they owed much. Epaphras was, in addition to being the "human" founder of the church there, a native of Colossae (see 4:12).

Colossians 1:9-14: Knowing how to divide these verses is not an easy matter. Some interpreters take verses 9-11 as a unit and begin a new section with verse 12. Others consider verses 3-14 as a single unit, and still others consider verses 9-14 as a separate entity. It seems best to follow the latter arrangement, for these verses seem to "hang together" and set the stage for the most controversial of all the passages in Colossians, namely, 1:15-20.

Paul now begins in earnest to lay the foundation for his arguments against the false teachers who emphasized so heavily the idea of "knowledge." He tells the Colossians that he is praying that they may be filled with "the knowledge of his [i.e., God's] will in all spiritual wisdom and understanding." The idea of "knowledge" has a particular meaning for Paul, with his Hebrew background, which differed from the Hellenistic sense. "Knowledge" in the Old Testament does not necessarily connote intellectual precepts, even though these may be a part of the overall picture. Rather, "knowledge" indicates a relationship between persons in whch each learns and grows and benefits from the relationship. The idea of the "knowledge of God" in the Old Testament, for example, means much more than simply knowing a few things about God. It means to enter into a relationship with God which is to be continuously experienced. This relationship teaches one what God requires (see Paul's "his will") and leads one into deeper wisdom and understanding, i.e., a fuller relationship with God.

These three terms—knowledge, wisdom, and understanding—could very well have been used by the "false teachers," for these were ideas used by the Hellenistic world but with very different meaning from Paul's usage of the words. Their kind of knowledge denoted primarily a certain intellectual knowledge of how the created order was structured. That gave, according to the Hellenistic world, wisdom and understanding. But Paul's meaning is that knowledge (that is, the right relationship with God) is the only knowledge that really brings true spiritual wisdom and understanding. The terms "wisdom and understanding" in this context could not then be used as means of boasting, as some of the "gnostic" believers did, taking pride and finding great security in "knowing" what others did not know.

Frequently for those who viewed the created order as basically evil and to be escaped, the material world was to be ignored. This could be done by either of two ways. One could attempt to escape it as much as possible, living an ascetic life-style so that one was "contaminated" as little as possible by it. Or one could simply ignore the world and its regulations. Since the material world does not really count for anything, there are no limitations or restrictions for anyone who has this esoteric knowledge. But one sees immediately that this is not the way Paul views the world, nor does he accept those kinds of ideas especially advocated by the libertines. He says that the true knowledge of God leads one into "a life worthy of the Lord" and further "increasing in the knowledge of God." This is an interesting point since intellectual knowledge which is totally self-contained has no "increasing" to do. But if "knowledge of God" represents a relationship with God, this makes good sense because relationships always are developing and growing.

There are several other points of interest in these verses, but the one that is most discussed concerns the idea of "the kingdom of his [God's] beloved Son." In the Synoptic Gospels (Matthew, Mark, and Luke) the kingdom is always referred to as God's kingdom. But once the church was established and was considered to be a part of the ministry of Jesus, the church began to think of the kingdom as belonging to Christ who would, at the consummation of that kingdom, present it to God. Paul argues for this point not only here but also in 1 Corinthians 15:24: "Then comes the end, when he [Christ] delivers the kingdom to God the Father after destroying every rule and every authority and power." The ideas in that passage are very close to the ideas which Paul now outlines in greater detail here in Colossians.

The last verse (14) of this section is also worthy of note. Paul declares emphatically that it is only through the beloved Son of God that redemption (i.e., release) is accomplished. It is interesting also that the Greek tense of the verb is a linear tense, i.e., indicating continuing action. Through Christ the Christian does not simply have a "saving" experience but actually continues to have day by day this same experience. Paul never believed in a religious experience that happened at one point in time in the Christian's life and then was over, the results always and forever valid. The Christian experience is one that is constantly and continuously renewed, day by day, because the present world with its power of sin and evil constantly beckons to one to return to the old ways. This is why so much of Paul's teaching is done in the exhortative style.

And further, from what is the Christian released? The false teachers at Colossae probably argued that it was from the power and dominion of this world order and the spiritual beings that ruled over the created order. But Paul realizes that it is not this group which exercises authority over and enslaves the human race. Sin does this! And God has dealt with human sin in the person and work of Christ. (One is reminded here of Matthew 1:20-21.) The way God has dealt with it is pointedly brought out in 1:20 and will be discussed more fully there.

Colossians 1:15-20: These verses are the most well known and also the most controversial of all in the letter to the Colossians. They have figured in some of the most bitter theological debates about the person of Jesus in the church (such as the Arian controversy in the fourth century A.D.), and more recently they have been the subject of great debate among New Testament scholars.

One of the chief critical questions discussed today about this passage revolves around whether these verses constituted a hymn of the early church in honor of the Christ. And, if so, what is the background and meaning and setting in the church of the original hymn, and how does Paul use and/or modify it? Most New Testament scholars today are convinced that these verses do reflect an early hymn, but unanimity of opinion is difficult to find after that initial agreement.

The problems are basically threefold: (1) What was the original structure of the hymn? (2) What was the origin of the hymn (in terms of background, Greek, Jewish, etc.)? (3) What function did it perform in the worship of the early church? These issues and discussions are far too complex and detailed for investigation here, but we shall attempt to point out some of the complexities involved.

First, there is the problem of how the hymn was originally structured. Some find that it had two basic *strophes* (roughly equivalent to stanzas), while others find that it had three. Some argue from the metrical structure of the hymn, while others argue from the content of the strophes.[1] It is interesting to note that in each reconstruction something has to be either omitted or shifted around to make the hymn a hymn!

If there is little agreement about the structure of the hymn, neither is there agreement on the origin and background of the hymn. Some argue that it is basically a Jewish hymn in honor of wisdom, adopted by the Christians and applied to Christ; others argue that it has a background in Greek gnostic thought closely related to the idea of a gnostic redeemer (i.e., a man from heaven who brings salvation to the world); and others argue that it was a creation of the early church.

What use did it serve in the church? Again there is much speculation but no assured agreement. The most widely accepted idea is that the hymn was used in the baptismal service when a new convert was being admitted into the fellowship of Christian believers. Or it could be that the hymn was simply used as a part of the worship service, possibly as a responsive reading, as an exaltation of the Lord of the church.

The problem is that all these theories are so complicated and complex as to make the reader wonder whether the hymn could ever have been either written or understood if all these manifold technicalities were involved in its origin. This is not to deny that there probably were many hymns written in the early church for use in various liturgical services, but I am not convinced that this passage contains a pre-Pauline hymn. The content of this passage is so clearly to the point of the problems facing the Colossian church that it seems more likely to have been written by Paul himself. The argument that the hymn is not in the Pauline style and it does not reflect Pauline language and vocabulary can be answered, it seems, rather easily. The fact that the passage is in hymnic or poetic form would mean that Paul is therefore writing in a style unusual and perhaps unnatural for him. And the vocabulary may well be different because the ideas and concepts with which he is dealing are different, reflecting the

[1] For the interested student, a brief summary of the material can be found in J. L. Houlden, ed., *Paul's Letters from Prison: Philippians, Colossians, Philemon and Ephesians* (Philadelphia: The Westminster Press, 1979), pp. 155-170.

specific problems in the Colossian church. That Paul can and sometimes does use hymns cannot be denied, and it seems fairly certain that he does just that in Philippians 2:6-11. But the present passage seems to be Paul's own effort to combat the false teachers with a "poem" of his own, probably suggested by other such hymns in the early church.

Having settled that issue once and for all (!), we nevertheless still need to examine a bit more closely the teachings that were probably causing the "heresy" which prompted this passage. As indicated in chapter 4, the problem here lay in the fact that these false teachers were arguing that Jesus was simply one of the "rulers of the universe." Since he was to be worshiped, should not all the others be worshiped also? Many Greeks believed that God was pure, unchangeable, spirit, and that as such he could not have created the impure, changeable, material world. How then did it come into existence? By a process of emanations (a kind of radiation from God) other beings were created. These beings were sometimes called *archons, rulers, principalities,* or *powers,* and were thought of as personal beings which exercised control over the created order. These beings had a relationship with one another and produced other beings like themselves in a descending order of progression. At the bottom of this superstructure, one (or possibly more than one) of these beings created the material world.

On the other hand, in Jewish thought, as it developed in the postexilic age (after 538 B.C.), there arose the idea of wisdom as God's agent in creation (see Job 28; Proverbs 8:22ff.; Psalm 33; as well as some intertestamental works). In fact, wisdom even became identified with the Torah (the Law). Also there arose in later Judaism a developed angelology, and it was believed that certain angels had certain functions. It was even argued that Moses received the Law through the angels instead of directly from God! These considerations have led some interpreters of Colossians to argue for a Jewish rather than a Greek background for the false teaching in Colossae.

There may be some truth in that argument, but the fact is that in some later gnostic circles (and probably in some earlier ones as well) the superstructure described above was called the *pleroma,* fullness. Since this is the very term which Paul uses in these verses (15-20) and later in 2:9, it seems more likely that the ideas being combated here are basically Greek in origin.

The interpretation of the verses is an interesting endeavor, because commentators do differ in some of their ideas concerning the exact meaning of this text. Perhaps it would be best to examine the text itself before attempting to make sense of the passage.

The first verse is aimed directly against those who would argue that Jesus is only one of a larger number of beings which act as intermediaries or buffers between the created order and God. Paul identifies Jesus as the "image of the invisible God, the first-born of all creation." One immediately is struck with the fact that Jesus is not far removed from God, but is the "first-born of all creation." The proper understanding of that term, "first-born of all creation," is not easy to determine. In the early church in the Arian controversy over the nature of Christ, the Arians interpreted this to mean that the Christ was a created part of the universe. And one can take the term "first-born" to designate a temporal event. But it is just as natural to understand the term in the sense of "authority," i.e., he is authoritative or supreme over all the created order. This seems to be the intent here especially in the light of some other considerations.

One of these considerations has to do with the meaning of the word "image." This term could apply to a physical likeness, but more often it was used in the sense of the representative of a king or person in authority who exercised the authority of the person who had sent him or her. The "image" represented the person who sent the delegate out and exercised the authority and purpose of the sender. In other words, Jesus as Son of God represents God to the human race. When one thinks about this idea, namely, that God has now revealed himself to the world in terms of a human personality, it is a staggering and sobering thought. Could there really be any higher revelation of God to the human race than that? Paul obviously understands the person of Jesus in this way. The meaning then of the "image" contains both the idea of revelation of God to the world and also the carrying out of God's purpose for the world (to which Paul comes in just a few verses).

It is difficult to be certain here *exactly* what Paul intends with this statement, but it seems clear that the key to understanding lies in the idea of Jesus as the "image" of God. As such, since he is the representative of God who acts with the authority of God, Jesus is indeed supreme ruler over the created order. And Paul goes on to list all those ideas, things, or beings which some were arguing had to be worshiped on an equal footing with the Christ. "He is before all things, and in him all things hold together." The word translated "hold together" literally means "stand together." In other words, the universe functions as God intends it to function as long as it acknowledges the sovereignty of God and God's representative. Otherwise it cannot stand!

At verse 18 Paul calls Jesus the "head of the body, the church." This is a slightly different analogy from that which he used in 1 Corinthians 12 (and Romans 12), but it is certainly not at variance with Paul's overall thought and indeed fits the context well here. Obviously Jesus' authority over the church was also being questioned, and Paul makes it clear that the church owes its allegiance to him. The reason for this is manifold. He is the "first-born from the dead," an obvious reference to the resurrection and the triumph over the great enemy of the human race, namely, death. But it is not simply physical death that is the "bugaboo" to the biblical writers. Physical death is basically a part of the created order and is not in itself considered a tragedy. If death comes too soon or by some horrible form, that would be a tragedy. But the real tragedy is the death which is the state of being apart from God. The biblical writers are quite clear that being apart from God is death, even if one is physically alive! The purpose of Jesus as the "image" of God was to give life to the human race, yea, even to the entire cosmos!

Verses 19-20 are crucial to the understanding of Paul's thought here as well. It is here in verse 19 that the term *pleroma,* fullness, is found, and scholars have argued for centuries about the exact meaning of that term. We have already seen that some interpreted the superstructure of the world to be a *pleroma,* and Paul is probably saying here that the *pleroma* does not exist—or if it does, it is contained in and is controlled by God's image, namely, Jesus the Christ. But the term probably is used in a much broader way than that, since it is God who is fully revealed in the Person of Jesus.

The main idea that is being emphasized by Paul (and it is sometimes missed by those who attempt to determine the exact and precise meaning of individual words) is the purpose of God's revelation in Jesus the Christ. "All the fulness of God" dwelt in Christ not simply to create a new being to worship, but for the purpose of accomplishing God's aim and goal for the world. This passage reflects the emphasis made in chapter 1 that the New Testament writers were more interested in the work of Christ than in his nature. God's purpose was to "reconcile to himself all things," and the Greek term for "all things" is emphatic that "all" in the sense of entirety is meant. This concept of reconciliation is a major point in Paul's religious thinking. He first emphasizes it in Second Corinthians (see 5:16-21) as he experiences a reconciliation with the people in the Corinthian church. And from that experience Paul understands somewhat more fully what reconciliation is all about, and from that understanding he is able to ascertain more clearly what God has done in and through the Person of the Christ.

It was accepted in the older Hebrew and Jewish thought that the fall of the human race brought not only enmity between God and humanity but also the corruption of the created order. So when God redeems the human race, creation will be redeemed as well. This is the idea Paul has in mind here (as well as in Second Corinthians and in Romans 8). Somehow through the cross, in the Person of Jesus in whom "God's fullness" dwelt, God has done something which will allow a reconciliation between the universe and God. The stage has been set for a new age in which God and the world can be one in the sense that the world is no longer angry at God and has its back turned upon him.

This entire passage (vv. 15-20) is so definitely Pauline and speaks so specifically to the situation at Colossae that it seems unlikely that Paul has used a preexisting hymn for this composition. It is not impossible nor even improbable that he used phrases or ideas already current in the churches of that day. But the composition as it stands seems to be quite Pauline.

Colossians 1:21-23: Paul now appeals to the Colossians to consider that they have already experienced the reconciling work of the Christ in their own lives. He describes how they were in their former state, "estranged and hostile in mind, doing evil deeds," but now they have been reconciled. And the emphasis here is upon the fact that the reconciliation was accomplished by God through his "image" and that image became identified with the "world of flesh" in which all live. The gnostics believed, of course, that God could not have any ·contact with the created world because it was essentially and inherently evil. Paul argues, however, that God has direct contact with the world in which we live and acts mightily to restore it to its proper place in the plan of God. There is no mythology here, only reality.

It is interesting to note that Paul again urges the recently committed Christians in the church there to "continue in the faith." The Greek is again emphatic at the point of continuing in a process; the Christians are being urged to remain constantly in the new relationship with God which has been made possible by the reconciling work of Christ.

One of the ways in which Paul differentiates between true religion and false religion is at the point of its scope. Is this teaching open and available for all people? Or is it only for the elite few? As far as Paul is concerned, this point is crucial. The Christian gospel is for "every creature under heaven," and Paul is genuinely grateful for the opportunity to be a participant in the proclamation of this "good news" (literally the word "gospel" in the Greek means "Good News") to all the world. And he urges them not to "shift away" from this gospel which they have heard and accepted.

Colossians 1:24–2:5: This section depicts a transition from the religious background and understanding to the specific problems (and Paul's answer to them) of the Colossian church.

First, Paul makes a rather peculiar statement, "in my flesh I complete what is lacking in Christ's afflictions for the sake of his body, that is, the church" (v. 24). This has caused interpreters some consternation, since some have understood Paul to mean that he is completing in some way the work of Christ on the cross, as if that work were incomplete. But it is obvious from a study of verses 15-20 that this meaning would be far from Paul's mind. Christ's work needed no one to complete it. Others have seen here in the reference to sufferings the events which would precede the Parousia, the return of Christ. In apocalyptic thought, which heavily influenced the church's understanding of the Parousia, a great persecution of God's people was expected during the period before the return. And in some apocalyptic works there was the idea of a completed portion of suffering or martyrdom which would have to transpire before the intervention of God and the destruction of the persecutors. Therefore, some argue, this idea is in Paul's mind at this point.

The overall context of the saying, however, does not appear to be related to the Parousia. It seems more to be Paul's own reflection about his ministry (to which he presently refers) and about his present status (imprisoned in Rome) than anything else. In many of Paul's letters he assumes that the lot of the Christian is to suffer. And since Christ suffered, should Christians be surprised that they are called upon to participate in that experience as well? There is no thought here of a "martyr complex," but rather the honest realization that Christians are different from the world and that the world will oppose them as vehemently, and at times perhaps even as violently, as it opposed *the* representative of God, namely, Jesus. Paul urges the Christian people to endure patiently the sufferings which would surely come upon them, realizing that this suffering can work toward good in the church and in the world as well as in the individual's life (see Romans 5:3ff.).

Paul, therefore, as a result of his acceptance of God's call to be a minister of the good news has had to suffer. And this suffering has been not only for God but for the sake of the building of the church as well.

Paul describes his ministry as a "divine office." There is some ambiguity at this point, for the word used in the Greek is *oikonomia,* which can have various meanings. Here, however, it seems to mean something like an "assignment" or a "special task," for he goes on to describe exactly how he understood his ministry, "to make the word of God fully known." But this "word" is described as a "mystery."

The term "mystery" in the world of Paul could have various meanings. In the gnostic-type settings the mystery could refer to the hidden knowledge of the superstructure of the world which would guarantee release from the created and evil world order. In fact there were numerous "mystery religions" in the Greco-Roman world which promised exactly that. But mystery could also mean something that had previously been hidden but had now been made public, i.e., revealed. It is in this sense that one usually finds the term used in Paul's writing, and this is probably the meaning intended here. It is again interesting that Paul can use a concept and idea of the false teachers and turn it against them. God's "hidden knowledge" is not to be restricted to a privileged few, but it is for all people. Not all people will recognize it for what it really is, but the "saints" will.

The "mystery" has been revealed through Jesus the Christ, and this mystery being accepted and appropriated by the people of God (which now includes the Gentiles) gives hope to and for the entire created order. In fact, some commentators think that the "mystery" is the inclusion of the Gentiles in God's plan. That is definitely part of what Paul has in mind, but "mystery" here is more appropriately understood as a reference primarily to Christ and his work. The idea of "glory" usually is limited to some aspect of God's "being" in the biblical texts, and quite often it designates God's presence with his people.

Here the term "hope of glory" probably is best understood as God's presence with his people, his transforming Presence which restores the original relationship established between God and humanity. This restoration cannot be fully accomplished in this world order, but the Christian has already experienced the "firstfruits" of the transforming relationship and looks forward to the full restoration in the future. Paul argues that Christ is proclaimed for this purpose to "present every man mature in Christ" (v. 28). This looks for and presupposes a period of growth in the Christian life.

The term "mature" is the translation of the Greek word *teleios,* which means "end" in the sense of a completed or accomplished task. It is the word from which we get the theological word "teleology," accomplishing a goal or purpose. It has the sense of "mature," grown to fullness and accomplishment, and it is the same word which is used in Matthew 5:48, "You, therefore, must be perfect [mature, complete, *teleios*], as your heavenly Father is perfect [*teleios*]." In other words one grows in the Christian faith to a point of completion and maturity. To bring people to this goal is Paul's consuming desire, for he believes with all his heart that God has called him for this purpose.

Even though Paul does not know these people in Colossae personally or directly, he feels an identification with them and a responsibility for them. It is his aim and purpose that they know (in the biblical sense) God and his mystery, Christ, and Paul argues rather strongly that in Christ all wisdom and knowledge are to be found. The idea of "hid" here has more the connotation of something being stored or deposited rather than being kept secret. All the treasures of wisdom and knowledge are contained in Christ.

Paul begins now to be more specific in his comments to the people at Colossae. His purpose in writing to them is that he does not want them to be deceived by people with smooth talk and easy solutions. And he exercises his position of authority in the church to "encourage" their "good order" and "firmness of faith" (2:5).

Colossians 2:6-15: Beginning at this point Paul now turns to the more specific problems facing the people in the church. He begins by exhorting them to "live in him [i.e., Christ]." The word translated "live" in the Greek literally means "walk around" and came to be used as an expression of one's life-style. How one "walked" indicated what kind of person one was and what kind of actions characterized one's life. Therefore when Paul urges the people to "live" in Christ, he is challenging them to exemplify in their daily "walk" the principles and precepts of the Christian faith and to demonstrate that the transforming power of God's Spirit truly is dwelling within them. It is also interesting to note that the verb tense in the Greek is again linear. It is not simply "live," but to "constantly and continuously live" in this manner. This is what they had been taught, and they had accepted the new life with thanksgiving. Therefore, do not turn away from this, Paul challenges them.

The crux of this entire section is probably to be found in 2:8. "See [the Greek says literally, "keep on the alert" and "continue to be aware"] to it that no one makes a prey of you [literally, "carries you off as a prize of war and enslaves"] by philosophy and empty deceit, according to human tradition, according to the elemental spirits of the universe, . . ." The verse carries a strong warning, urging the people to be constantly on guard against those who would like to capture them by means of "philosophy and empty deceit." Exactly what Paul means by "philosophy" cannot be determined, but it appears to have direct connection with the idea of the alleged "superior" knowledge which the false teachers were espousing. Paul identifies it as "empty deceit."

The second part of this verse emphasizes Paul's opposition not only to this particular problem in Colossae but also to a similar problem which plagues the entire world. What is wrong is that people everywhere have accepted as genuine what is in reality only human tradition. What has been revealed in Christ, however, transcends the traditions of the world, and these traditions stand in opposition to the progress which is available through God's action in Christ. These human traditions are closely identified with the "elemental spirits of the universe."

Most commentators interpret the Greek term *stoicheia*, "elemental spirits of the universe," in this way. And the word did frequently designate the rulers of the spirit world, usually meaning the evil spirit world! These were interpreted as demonic powers which hold sway over the lives of people in this world. It is interesting that Paul taunts the false teachers by saying that their very teaching which claims to release people from bondage to these spirits in fact makes them even more enslaved to those very elements! The word, however, can have another meaning. It can denote primitive or elemental thinking—in this case, religious thinking. If this is the case here, Paul would be arguing against primitive religious ideas found among the human race. It is unlikely that this is intended here, at least primarily, but the double meaning might well be what Paul had in mind.

Again Paul reiterates what he has emphatically stated before. In Christ dwells the "whole fulness of deity" (2:9). He probably intends the same meaning here as in 1:19-20, even though the wording used in this verse is somewhat different. The emphasis in this statement is upon "in him." What abides "in him" is the whole fullness of "deity."

This is a strong term probably representing all the power and sovereignty which belong to God. But the key word here appears to be "bodily." What does this mean?

We are reminded again of the fact that Paul, as any writer, can use words with more than one meaning. But, as with many of Paul's favorite words, there is a primary meaning which he seems to designate most usually for the word "body." The term can denote the physical body. This is a usual and obvious designation. But Paul seems to indicate something more in his usage of the word. The Hebrew way of viewing the makeup of a human being was quite different from certain Greek thought. To many Greeks the "body" was an evil prison that held captive the good "spirit." This represents a type of dichotomy between flesh and spirit which is not found in the Old Testament. There we find that human beings are viewed as "whole" persons, composed of a physical body and a spiritual (or psychological) dimension fused together into a single entity. Paul seems definitely to be governed by this basic understanding of the human element in creation, and it explains why he does not view "flesh" or the material world as inherently evil in itself as did the gnostic speculators. His use of the term "body" then seems to reflect this idea. The body designates for Paul the essential characteristics of a person, what makes a person as she or he is. Today the term "selfhood" may be somewhat similar, indicating the whole being or personality. This understanding assists in making sense of several difficult passages in Paul (see, for example, 1 Corinthians 6:15-20; 15:35-50).

In this passage here in Colossians Paul, by the use of the term "bodily," emphasizes again that in Jesus the essential qualities and functions of God reside, especially as these relate to the reconciliation process. And as a result of this those who have committed their lives to him find fullness of life.

The next few verses seem to be an analogy using the rite of baptism to illustrate the difference between the old life (dead in trespasses) and the new life (forgiven and delivered from the enslaving forces). This use of the figure of baptism is the reason some interpreters argue for a baptismal ritual for the setting of much of these first two chapters. But Paul has used the figure of baptism in another place as simply illustrative (see Romans 6:1-11), and there seems to be no reason to argue for such a specific setting here.

Again Paul argues that God has forgiven sin and has defeated the worst power of evil in and through the cross. Not only has he defeated

the forces of evil, but also he has made "a public example of them."
Even though the meaning of the figure is not absolutely certain to
interpreters, the intent of the idea of "nailing [the charge which stood
against us] to the cross" seems clear. God has forgiven the sins of the
human race, thereby making it possible for reconciliation to occur—
if only people will accept it.

Colossians 2:16-23: It is in this passage that we face the direct and
specific activities advocated by the false teachers in Colossae.
Obviously there was an emphasis on eating (or not eating) certain
food and keeping certain rituals related to festivals (possibly pagan),
new moons (pagan and Jewish), and sabbaths (basically Jewish).
These were almost certainly related to the worship of angels and other
"powers." But Paul urges the people not to lose sight of the Head who
holds the church together and causes it to grow.

Paul's concern is intense because the false teaching is leading
directly to "false living." Worship of these "elements" of the universe
cannot be categorized as anything other than idolatry. And, further,
Christians are supposed to have been released from the keeping of
external regulations and the tyranny which accompanies
such activity (see Galatians 5:1). The stipulations "Do not handle, Do
not taste, Do not touch" seem to reflect a type of ascetic
understanding to shun anything material in this world. Doing these
things as a means of assuring the "spirituality" of the person pursuing
these practices is deceptive and self-defeating. Such actions cause
false pride and do not really check the "indulgence of the flesh." Here
the meaning of the term "flesh" is given its usual Pauline nuance, i.e.,
that state in which humanity finds itself apart from God. And this
means that "flesh" denotes much more than simply physical items
(see Galatians 5:16-24). Therefore, asceticism for the sake of
asceticism, trying thereby to win favor before God, is simply another
way of making an idol. The Jews had done this with the Law (see
Romans 2 for only one example); Gentiles have done the same type of
thing with extreme asceticism. But such activity cannot accomplish
what the gift of God in Christ did, granting this new life to all who will
accept it.

This passage reflects again the human tendency to want to do
everything "right" and to know "everything" to assure "salvation."
There is in such activity and attitude the human search for security,
ironclad security which *guarantees* certain results. Many persons
approach any religion with this in mind, but the religion of the Bible,

and especially the religion of Paul, has no such understanding. The first sin resulted from wanting to know everything and to become "gods" (see Genesis 3:5). Abraham, when he was called, went out trusting God but not knowing where he went (see Genesis 12 and Hebrews 11:8ff.)! Faith always has a degree of uncertainty and insecurity in it; otherwise it is not faith.

Colossians 3:1-17: This rather lengthy section contains a long series of exhortations directed toward the Christian who is struggling with the world as well as false teaching. The passage can be divided into three divisions, verses 1-4, 5-11, and 12-17.

In verses 1-4 Paul immediately sets out the basis for the Christian life. Unfortunately this point is often obscured by the translation which should read, "*Since* you have been raised with Christ." There is no indication here of any doubt or hesitancy, and the Greek construction makes that point very clear. And *since* Christians have been raised with Christ, this places them in a new position with regard to God. And quite normally for Paul, he launches into a series of exhortations and admonitions challenging the Christian people "to seek constantly and continuously the things that are above," constantly and continuously setting their minds and wills in a different order from that of the world. It is probably certain that verse 4 refers to the time of the Parousia, and it is a reassurance to the people that their efforts will not be in vain.

In the second division (vv. 5-11) Paul urges the people to set aside the old ways of the world. "Put [them] to death." This is not an appeal for a rigid asceticism, for this is one of the ideas Paul is challenging with regard to the false teachers at Colossae. But there are certain attitudes of life which are incompatible with the Christian way. The list which Paul cites here concludes with "covetousness, which is idolatry." Elsewhere in Paul's writings he makes much of the idea of covetousness (see Romans 7:7-8) which seems to epitomize for him the fundamental sin of the human race. The term seems to indicate in Paul's mind the idea that the selfish ego of the personality considers itself to be *the* greatest entity in the universe and sees itself as so important that it can use all other things and all other persons as simply instruments for its pleasure (note that the other four terms in the list relate to sexual vices). This is idolatry, the worship of self and gratification of what the old self apart from God wants! But the Christian is supposed to have been killed to self and raised with Christ to a new order with new directions and purpose and with a new center for life, namely, God. The list reflects some of the pagan morality—the times are not that different today!

The wrath of God comes upon those who practice such things. It is interesting that many interpreters take verse 6 to be a reference to the final judgment. And this is quite probably intended. But Paul does not, as the prophets before him did not, limit God's wrath and judgment to the end time. The verb in the Greek is again a present tense indicating an ongoing process of judgment (see Romans 1:18-32) which is not limited simply to one time or one place.

In verse 8 there is another list describing certain attitudes which the Christian is to "put away." The reader is struck with the fact that there are again five items in the list. It is interesting to note that Paul sees clearly the damage that lying causes. In such a situation there can be no real trust, love, or commitment among the members of the Christian community. And that community is supposed to be the body of Christ characterized by a loving and trusting relationship among all the members and in each member.

In the idea here of putting off the old nature and putting on the new nature, scholars again see a reference to baptism. Whether Paul is using the rite itself as absolute or whether he is using it analogously (i.e., as a comparison to make a point) can be debated. The latter view is taken here. What is important is the description of the new nature. It is "renewed in knowledge after the image of its creator." We have already discussed the basic meaning of "knowledge" and of "image"; and if one keeps these definitions in mind, the meaning of the text becomes clear. The new relationship with God creates a new humanity through the "image" [who is Christ] which reveals and restores the original purpose of God in creation.

Paul likes to use the figure comparing the old nature and the new nature, and he usually does this by speaking about the "old Adam" and the "new Adam." This passage reflects that Pauline motif (see Romans 5:12ff.; 1 Corinthians 15:45ff.; possibly Philippians 2:6-8). And it is well to note that Paul uses these terms not so much individualistically but rather corporately. It is an old community being compared and contrasted with a new community. And in the new community the old distinctions are done away. "Here there cannot be Greek and Jew, circumcised and uncircumcised, barbarian, Scythian, slave, free man, but Christ is all, and in all."

The reference here to a "Scythian" is puzzling to many interpreters. Paul has used the method of contrasting elements before to emphasize the oneness of Christians together and the fact that all people are invited to become participants in this new life (see Galatians 3:28). But the Scythian appears to be an "intruder" into this listing. These people were members of rather primitive and savage tribes which lived along the Black Sea. From these people came many slaves in the Greco-Roman world. Couple this with the fact that Paul later devotes a disproportionate amount of space to slaves and masters, and one becomes puzzled as to why such emphasis should be given to this area.

It is possible that in the listing in 3:11 that Paul is simply attempting to give as broad as possible a cross-listing of all peoples and types who may have made up the Colossian church. This is quite logical. But there may be a more pressing reason. We are reminded that this letter was sent at the same time and to the same place as the letter to Philemon in which Paul is literally pleading for the life of the runaway slave, Onesimus. The emphasis then in this writing concerning slaves may well be a result of the fact that this matter is now pressing so intently on Paul's mind. The emphasis in Colossians about this area of Christian relationships and responsibilities becomes understandable in this light.

This section is then followed by another (vv. 12-17) in which there is another list containing five items, this time "virtues" rather than "vices." There are to be certain characteristics of the Christian life-style that set the Christian apart from the world as it is in its harsh reality. Paul never argues that Christians can fully keep the commands of Jesus, but he does argue that there are certain principles of conduct which can and should become "part and parcel" of a Christian's life. And it is interesting to note that forgiveness is emphasized here (another reference to the slave, Onesimus?).

In verse 15 the people are again challenged to let "the peace [i.e., well-being] of Christ [constantly and continuously] rule in your hearts." The word translated "rule" is much more rich in meaning than that. The term can have either legal or athletic connotations, and in this case the athletic metaphor is probably correct, for Paul was very fond of using athletic images. The word indicates something of a judge or an official giving guidance or a ruling which can change the course of the game. The word here probably came to mean something like "exercise control over." One's life is to be governed by the peace of Christ in such a way as to change not only the direction of the individual's life but the life of the church and society as well.

And Paul always reminds the people at Colossae as elsewhere "to be thankful." This term is also a challenge for a constant and continuous process of "becoming" thankful, which is the more literal translation of the Greek. Far too often persons who have been blessed by good fortune or are the objects of mercy fail to remember to be grateful (see Matthew 18:23-35).

Again there is, in verse 16, the challenge to "let the word of Christ" constantly and continuously dwell in the one called to be with Christ. These gifts of grace are to be used for supporting, sustaining, and exalting one's Christian neighbors. We get a brief glimpse in verse 16 into the importance of psalms and songs in the life of the early church—as they have been through the centuries. Everything is to be done in the "name of the Lord Jesus." Persons today quite frequently miss the real impact of this idea. The "name" in biblical times was believed to carry within itself something of the essential nature of the person. Therefore, doing something in the "name" of someone else really meant to be doing something in the "essential nature" of that person. The meaning should be quite clear. Christians are to reflect in themselves the essential nature and qualities of the Head of the church. This is the proper way for persons to demonstrate their gratitude to God for his gracious action on their behalf through Christ (v. 17).

Colossians 3:18–4:1: Paul at this point inserts a list of "household" duties. Such lists were not uncommon in the pagan and Jewish background of that time. The question arises as to why Paul would insert it at this point, and, further, why the largest portion is devoted to the slave-master relationship. One is again reminded of the Onesimus affair and Paul's attempt to do what was right and proper (according to Roman law) by sending the runaway slave back to his master, while at the same time protecting Onesimus from the wrath of Philemon. In order to place more pressure on Philemon, Paul inserts here a brief discussion of social duties and responsibilities accepted by the society of that time. But he, nevertheless, interprets these social relationships as having been transformed for those within the Christian community.

There are those who have faulted Paul for his "conservatism" at this point, arguing that if Paul were indeed the great liberated thinker he is made out to be, he would have argued for the absolute equality of husband and wife and for the immediate emancipation of every slave. It is all too easy to view Paul in this light. But there are numerous facts that should also be kept in mind before one becomes hypercritical of the great apostle.

First of all, it must be remembered that every age of human history has social and cultural contexts, not all of which are totally "good, acceptable, and perfect." Not even our own "enlightened" age can claim perfection. There have to be, in order for there to be an orderly society (in which there is stability and the opportunity for progress), certain accepted lines of authority. Without such lines of authority there is no stability in the society and chaos results. The lines of authority will not be the same in every age or every society. The cultural background with which the apostle Paul had to deal was in some ways no better and no worse than our own! And unless he became either a recluse or a social revolutionary, these were aspects of the world with which he had to live.

Secondly, even though certain aspects of his culture were "given," Paul clearly understood these kinds of social relationships to stand transformed under the power of the Spirit of God. Paul's Jewish background, for example, would have no part of women meddling in religion except as observers and helpers, doing what they were told! But Paul, when he became a Christian, practiced an equality between the sexes rarely seen even in the history of the church! Some of his most trusted co-workers were women (see Romans 16:1, 3). And in a time when the husband was considered to be "lord and master of the wife," one is stunned to read in 1 Corinthians 7:4: "For the wife does not rule over her own body, but the husband does; likewise the husband does not rule over his own body, but the wife does." A more "equal" statement could not be made! And he does not, even though he is often quoted to the contrary, advocate that women should not be allowed to speak in church. He explicitly states in 1 Corinthians 11:2ff. that women could both preach and pray in the public worship. (For a consideration and proper understanding of those other passages, the reader is referred to a good commentary to explain the background and reasons for his statements there.) It is therefore very clear that Paul understands the Christian life-style to transform existing social standards, at least within the Christian fellowship.

Lastly, there is also the added dimension of how Paul thinks about the Parousia. The early church believed that Jesus would return *soon,* within their lifetime, and Paul certainly accepts that tenet of the church. In 1 Corinthians 7, for example, he argues (in response to a question put to him by the church) that people are better off not to marry. This is not because he believes that sexual relations are evil; he specifically states that they are not (done in the proper context, of course). He does not believe that a celibate life is "higher" than a noncelibate life. His argument is based squarely on his belief that the Parousia will come shortly. And the accepted scheme for this event was typically apocalyptic in outline: a time of intense persecution of the people of God, followed by the intervention of God to destroy the persecutor. In the thought of the early church the return of Jesus was the intervention of God. In such a time of intense suffering, Paul argues that it is better not to have any additional duties or responsibilities such as one always has in the marriage relationship. And further, one would certainly not want to have children and have them suffer in the intense persecution.

Thus the advice Paul gives to the people at Corinth is not an absolute doctrine for all times and all places, but practical advice based upon his understanding of the historical moment. And at that point in time he argues that it is better not to marry and have sexual relations. (There certainly could conceivably be periods in which this advice might still be quite sound, but not in "normal" situations.) This advice, given to the Corinthians but which "sounds" different from Colossians, has led some interpreters of Paul to argue that by the time he wrote the Colossian letter, his idea about the Parousia had changed and that he had given up any hope of its imminent occurrence. But this is really to miss the point. Paul is not here basically arguing for a long-range mode of living, but is rather using the ideas current at that time up to the point about Onesimus. His very brief reference here to the family situation does not necessarily imply that his mind has changed about the Parousia. One recalls that in 3:4 he has explicitly referred to Jesus' appearance.

This specific passage, then, has several interesting points to make. Paul assumes that in the family situation at that moment of social history the husband is the appropriate authority. But the husbands are urged to "love" their wives (one notes again the Greek tense denoting continuous and constant action), and one cannot but be reminded that "love" did not at that time have as much to do with marriage as it supposedly does today.

Parents were, of course, to have authority over the children; with that our culture even today still basically agrees. In Paul's time children were not given "center stage" as they sometimes are in our present society. The authority of the parent was considered fairly absolute. But Paul again places the one in authority in a position also of responsibility urging parents not to "provoke" their children. The word used by Paul needs some further explication. It carries the meaning of nagging or berating. What is intended is for the parent to treat the child in such a way that the child is strengthened and developed positively, not cowed, discouraged, or browbeaten so that the child's self-esteem is destroyed. This is again a rather advanced idea for that time.

But the main purpose of this section is to discuss the relationship between masters and slaves. We have already noted the background for this with the Onesimus-Philemon problem. Paul begins by urging slaves (and there were probably quite a few slaves who were Christians) to obey their earthly masters. And he urges them to do this not simply by external appearance but in real depth and labor. If so, they will not need to fear their masters and will also please the Lord. Paul seems to feel that honest work is not to be shunned but entered into as a part of pleasing God no matter what one's status in life. One recalls Paul's own adamant struggle to support himself to set an example (see 2 Thessalonians 3:7f.; 1 Corinthians 9:1-15, among others) for those in the church.

The masters are then challenged to treat their slaves "justly and fairly," for they are reminded that they along with all others must stand the judgment of God. Some persons are at times perturbed at Paul for not using this occasion as a platform for an emancipation proclamation! But one must remember that Paul is not here seeking to establish a principle forever, but to save a man's life. And it is also the case that a slave uprising in those days would have been most viciously and cruelly crushed. There is ample evidence of this from secular sources of that time. In spite of his failure to attempt to rally a slave revolt, Paul, nevertheless, laid the solid foundation for the equality of all people. Since we live in a world that does not always understand or appreciate such enlightened ideas, it sometimes is a manifestation of true "wisdom" to know what can be done realistically. Unfortunately the world will not be transformed overnight; not even dedicated Christians can be!

Colossians 4:2-6: As a summary of 3:1-4:1, Paul challenges the Colossian Christians to continue in prayer and asks that they remember him (as he is in prison at that moment) and his work in their prayers. He urges them especially to set a good example for those outside the Christian fellowship. (The Christian life is still perhaps the most potent witness to the faith which can be made.) They should be "gracious" to others in their speech; he even argues that their speech be "seasoned with salt." This metaphor probably means that what they say is to act as that which brings out the very best in meaning from every situation, not necessarily simply being jovial or lively or "spicy." The Colossians are challenged to make the "most of the time," probably a reference to the time until the Parousia, but commentators differ in their interpretation of this phrase. It is clearly a challenge to them to use every opportunity to witness to their faith.

Colossians 4:7-18: We have come now to the conclusion of this letter, where Paul tells the people of his plans and sends personal greetings to many. He tells us that Tychicus is the one who will bring the letter to Colossae and that he will be accompanied by the runaway slave, Onesimus (see the letter to Philemon). Others are also named as sending their good wishes to the people of the church.

There is the interesting statement at verse 16 about exchanging letters with the church at Laodicea. The letter from Laodicea has, in all probability, been lost to us. We also get a glimpse into the size of these early churches; they meet in someone's house!

And finally, there is the reference to Archippus who may be a member of Philemon's household, or more probably the leader of the church there. He is mentioned also in Philemon, verse 2, and the challenge to "fulfill his ministry" may be Paul's challenge for him to see to it that Philemon does what is right by Onesimus. But this is really only conjecture.

Paul concludes the letter by writing a brief note "in my own hand." Most of his letters were dictated to someone who wrote them down for him.

Even though Paul did not know these people personally, he certainly gave to them a marvelous proclamation of faith, a challenge to live as true Christians, and a magnificent description of the one who is Lord of the church!

6   Ephesians—
An Exposition

The New Testament writing which has been known for centuries as Paul's letter to the Ephesians is a masterpiece of literary style and religious meaning. As has already been discussed (see pp. 46-51), there are some very real problems in seeking to determine some of the historical background for the writing of this letter. If one accepts the tradition, the letter was written by Paul from prison (probably in Rome) about A.D. 62 to the churches in and around Ephesus. We definitely know that the letter was not originally addressed "to the Ephesians" since those words are not in the earliest Greek manuscripts of this writing and since also it was known in the early second century as the "Letter to the Laodiceans." Therefore, in all probability it was a document directed toward a group of churches in a given area (probably in Asia Minor), and it ultimately became identified with the chief church in that area, namely, the church at Ephesus.

There are, however, some very real problems with accepting this letter as genuinely from the hand of Paul. There are vocabulary differences, stylistic differences, and theological differences, but no one of these arguments by itself could carry enough decisive weight to cast absolute doubt on Pauline authorship. It is rather the combination of these elements which seems weighty in this matter together with the fact that there are in Ephesians certain historical assertions and assumptions which fit better into the later period of Christian church history, especially the period after A.D. 70. Until this date the Christians were basically considered to be simply a sect movement within Judaism. But with the capture of Jerusalem by the Romans in A.D. 70 and the destruction (or at least partial destruction) of the temple there, and with the growth of the Christian movement especially among the Gentiles, the church and the synagogue came to be two separate and distinct entities. And as the years rolled by, the great controversy in the church about the relationship between Jew and Gentile subsided. This had not fully transpired within Paul's lifetime. Further, we know from the traditions of the church that both Paul and Peter were martyred in Nero's persecution of the Christians in Rome, about A.D. 65. If, indeed, there are in the letter to the Ephesians references to a second generation of Christians, this must be understood as a period of time later than Paul. We shall attempt to point out such references in the exposition of the book itself.

But if the letter reflects a time later than Paul, questions abound. Who wrote this magnificent piece of religious literature? Why? Where? The reader is again referred to the specific discussions of these matters already addressed (see pp. 46-51). But a brief summary of the assumptions which will serve as the basis for our exposition of the book would not be inappropriate to include at this point.

It is assumed here that the writing known to us as the letter to the Ephesians reflects a later historical period than that of the apostle Paul. Therefore, the book is a pseudonymous work, written by an ardent admirer of Paul to summarize Paul's thinking for his own time and place. The writer obviously lived in a period of time when the church was having difficulty in understanding its place in the overall purpose of God for the world. This feeling would have been keenly felt in the post-apostolic period when the problem of the delay in the Parousia troubled the people in the church and lay open for them the question of the role of the church over a "long-range" period of time. This writer wanted to explain to the church of his own time something about its existence—its leader, its purpose, its composition, and its challenge.

But the question still remains. If Paul did not write this treatise, who did? We have already been made aware of the conjecture that it was Onesimus, the slave about whom Paul wrote in Philemon (and probably Colossians). This makes some sense, for certainly Onesimus would have had much to be thankful for in the life, ministry, and writings of Paul. We have seen, however, that there is no real guarantee that the Onesimus who was bishop at Ephesus about A.D. 110-115 was the same Onesimus Paul wrote about. And even if he were, is it really likely that he composed a work as masterfully done as Ephesians? It is possible, but it is highly improbable. Some few have guessed that it may have been Tychicus, the person who delivered the letters to the Colossians and to Philemon, and who, interestingly enough, is mentioned in Ephesians 6:21 (see Colossians 4:7ff.). This could explain the author's admiration for Paul and also the heavy dependence on Colossians and Philemon found in this letter. But again this is conjecture!

There could possibly be a good case made for Timothy (or some other of Paul's co-workers) as the writer of this book. We know that Timothy had some Jewish background (many feel that the author of Ephesians had a Jewish background); he was closely connected with Paul's work in Ephesus (see 1 Timothy 1:3) and was, frankly, Paul's chief and most trusted assistant. Who else would have been so closely associated with Paul's overall thought? But this too is conjecture!

All that can be said with any degree of certainty is that whoever the author of this treatise was, he loved Paul and the church, and he wrote to explain to the church of his time (and all time) its reason for being.

Ephesians 1:1-2: The form of this writing is that of a formal letter though no specific place or group of people is named. It is interesting that the salutation names only Paul as the author. There are no others mentioned, as is usually the case.

We have already mentioned the fact that the words in verse 1, "at Ephesus," known to us from older traditions, do not occur in the oldest Greek texts. This has led some to argue that the letter originally was a circular letter; the author perhaps even left a blank space at this point in the writing so that the appropriate church designation could be inserted, depending upon where the letter was being read at that moment. This is possible, but not likely. The letter is simply addressed "to the saints who are also faithful in Christ Jesus," i.e., those who have committed their lives in the trust commitment necessary to become a participant in the church of Christ.

The salutation concludes with the familiar "grace . . . and peace." (See the discussion on Colossians 1:1-2.)

Ephesians 1:3-14: At this point in Paul's letters we usually find a section in which Paul gives thanks for the people to whom he is writing as well as for many other gifts which God has given to him and to the world. Here, however, we have a long sentence (these verses in the Greek are indeed only *one* sentence!) set in the form of a blessing. This has led some to interpret these verses as a kind of liturgical piece, perhaps used by the early church in connection with the baptismal ritual. But these verses are so much like the remainder of Ephesians that they are unlikely to have been composed by a different author. The style may appear to be liturgical in nature, because this author seems to be "at home" with this style of literary composition.

One is hard pressed to be able to make evident to the reader who does not know Greek just how flowing and majestic these verses are in the original. They are full of participles and phrases begun by "of the . . ." which simply seem to flow in an unending stream building up to a climax of words and meanings which simply inundate the hearer (or the reader) with their brilliance. The translations most well known to us break these verses into shorter sentences. But in the Greek they flow in such a manner that one thought seems not to be finished until another is rolling in over the top of the one preceding it!

This passage sets the stage for the entire book. Many have argued that the great theme of Ephesians is the unity of the church. Others have argued for the centrality of Jesus the Christ as the unifying factor in the writing. Even though these aspects are truly emphasized in and through this treatise, as well as are other themes, the one integrating item is that of God and his plan for the world. The Christ, the church, and all other important matters have their origin and owe their being to the God who is the "Father of the Lord Jesus Christ." It is because of God and God's action on behalf of us all that the author of Ephesians devoutly begins with a poem of praise to God.

The flow of the argument logically turns almost immediately to the reason for this ascription of praise. It is because God "has blessed us in Christ." The term "in Christ" probably means here "by means of Christ" (this is not the usual Pauline meaning). What has occurred is that the Christian has been blessed with "every spiritual blessing." Exactly what that means is probably to be found in the following statements: The Christian has been chosen to be with God, and to be with God means that many responsibilities are now part of the Christian's life. Christians can stand before God because God has redeemed them, i.e., forgiven their sins (vv. 4-8).

There is another item of interest in these first few verses. Jesus is called the "one beloved." The Greek is translated simply "the Beloved." The important point here is that this term was never used by Paul to apply to Jesus. Echoes of the term are found in the stories of Jesus' baptism (see Mark 1:11, and parallels) and perhaps in Colossians 1:13. But the term as it is used here in Ephesians to refer to Jesus as God's Messiah did not come into vogue in the early Christian church until the end of the first century A.D. and the beginning of the second.

There is something of a problem for the interpreter in attempting to determine the exact translation of verses 8 and 9. Because of the flowing style of this author, it is sometimes difficult to know exactly where to place certain words in a translation. For example, the literal meaning of verse 8 is, "which he has lavished upon us in all [every] wisdom and insight." The question is whether to place "wisdom and insight" with "lavished" or to place it with "has made known" at the beginning of verse 9. Is it that God has lavished his grace upon us in "all wisdom and insight," emphasizing his own plan (as the author of Ephesians certainly does seem to do), or does the passage mean that God has made known to us "in all wisdom and insight" the mystery of his will? Certainty cannot be assured, but the first seems to fit the context and the grammatical style better than the latter possibility, for which the RSV translators opted.

Another problem here lies in the meaning of the word "mystery." In the letter to the Colossians the term referred to Christ, but here in Ephesians it seems to imply God's plan of redemption which had long been hidden from the minds of human beings but has now been revealed in the work of Jesus. This plan is for all things to be united in him. "All things" here obviously refers not simply to reconciliation between God and people and people and people but to all there is in the created order. And the word translated "unite" really means to "sum up" or "recapitulate," "to re-center," perhaps with the idea of bringing all creation back into the original status which it had with God in the beginning! And this he is accomplishing through the work of Jesus who was sent at "the fulness of time." There is an order and structure involved in God's dealing with the world in the work of redemption, i.e., setting people and the universe free from enslavement to sin.

It is interesting to note that in verses 11-14 persons are divided into those who "first hoped" and then "you also who have heard." This seems to indicate a distinction between the time of the alleged writer, Paul, and the Christian group which is now being addressed, hardly a thought which would have come from Paul's time.

The passage here under consideration is so full of the richness of God's activity on behalf of his people that it is impossible in such a short exposition to begin to do justice to the text. The emphasis is upon God's initiating action and his ultimate plan for the universe which is to be accomplished through the work of Christ. The author wants to make it clear that the results of this plan and Christ's activity have brought "salvation" to those who will commit themselves in faith to that goal. The gift of the Spirit is the "guarantee" or "down payment" of the ultimate riches which are to be finalized and completed for the Christian. And all of this is "to the praise of his glory."

Ephesians 1:15-23: This section (again one long sentence) begins as a thanksgiving but quickly evolves into another marvelous exposition of the glory of God and the mind-staggering plan and purpose which will be accomplished through the church. What Christ accomplished on behalf of the world and the Christians is beyond human comprehension. One interesting point to note here is that the emphasis is upon the triumph over death. The phrase "the riches of his glorious inheritance in the saints" quite probably refers not to angels, as some argue, but rather to those Christians who have gone before and have now reached their reward in the "heavenly places."

The reader is struck by the absolute certainty with which this writer presents his convictions. But it is not by human thought or will or action that these things are and will be accomplished—it is through the majesty of this God supreme over all creation. And not only are these goals accomplished in and through the Christ, but in and through the church as well. Here the word "church" does not refer to a local congregation, as it usually does in Paul's writings, but the church universal, the church militant and the church triumphant, for this writer does not see any discontinuity between the two!

Ephesians 2:1-10: The author has just described the majesty of God, the plan for the universe to be accomplished through Christ and his church, and the privilege which one has of being called to be a part of this challenging promise of hope. He now describes the state of those apart from God, and how one escapes from this morass of sin. Those apart from God are dead in "trespasses [deliberate acts of sin] and sins" (the natural state of doing wrong things, possibly out of ignorance). Being dead in the biblical sense normally implies a "spiritual death" rather than physical death, and this is the meaning here. It is clear that the author thinks that this is the "normal" state of the human race (v. 4) apart from God.

But God has "made us alive together with Christ." And this action was done even "when we were dead through our trespasses [committing deliberate acts of sin against God's law]." At this point the author inserts a curious and short clause which we would probably designate as a parenthetical expression: "By grace you have been saved." The words are abrupt and also interesting.

Paul almost never (only once and in a special sense) uses the verb "to save" in a past tense. His usual way of expressing God's activity on our behalf in the past is to use a form of the Greek verb "to justify." And the verb "to save" is most often found in the future and less frequently in the present. The verb form used here designates an action completed in the past with the results of that action continuing into the present. The idea seems to emphasize that God's act in Christ (grace) and the Christian's acceptance of that act and commitment to it (faith) produce the new life which one can call "being saved."

This act places the Christian in a different position with regard to God and the world. The resurrection of Christ is, in the New Testament writings, a proclamation of the emergence of a new kind of life in this old world order. It is a new life characterized by the presence of God in the very being of the one committed to the Christ. (This is probably the intent of verse 6.) And it is the kind of life that continues through the "coming ages." One notes here that the reference to "coming ages" is quite different from an expectation of an early return of Jesus.

The next verses (8-9) to a great degree summarize Paul's basic religious understanding. People are in a situation from which they cannot extricate themselves. They do not deserve nor can they earn the forgiveness and reconciliation which must take place before they can receive new life. God, out of his love and mercy, did for them what they could not do for themselves. The emphasis here is upon God's action in the process.

Another curious phrase then occurs here. The author of Ephesians states that the Christian is created "by means of Christ Jesus *upon* good works" (my translation). The word "upon" is usually translated as "for" in the modern versions, but the Greek word used here primarily means "on, in, upon, above." It can mean something like "for the purpose of" but this is usually designated (especially in Paul's letters) by the Greek word *eis*. A second item of interest is the phrase "good works." It would be peculiar, indeed, to hear Paul use such a term. This is not because Paul was opposed to or apathetic about "good works," far from it, but Paul was for so long battling against a mind-set that attempted to gain God's favor by committing "works." And he usually was very reluctant to speak of "works" except in a negative sense. By the latter stages of the first century A.D., however, the phrase "good works" seems to have become accepted for acts of kindness and compassion.

The passage, therefore, seems to reflect the meaning which the RSV translators gave to it, but there seems to be also another dimension which is frequently overlooked. The author of Ephesians has just argued that salvation has come only through the grace and free gift of God and not through "works." He then states that Christians are his "workmanship, created in Christ Jesus [above] good works." In other words, the emphasis here is that "good works" have absolutely nothing to do with the free act of God in Christ to redeem human beings. But the author quickly adds (and Paul himself would have agreed) that once this new creation has taken place, "good works" become characteristic of those who have been re-created. While salvation does not come *because* of good works, it does not come apart from good works. There are certain characteristics of the newly created people of God which set them apart from the ordinary world of humankind.

Ephesians 2:11-22: The author now turns his attention directly to the Gentiles, who he seems to assume constitute the vast majority of the church. The greatness of God and of his activity is shown in the fact that there are no longer two divisions of people in the world but only one. The tone of this section seems to reflect a pleading with the Gentile church not to forget that it was from Judaism that God's revelation and activity came. It could have been that the church at the time of the writing of this letter had begun to lose any sense of its origins, and this can be disastrous to any institution. History is important, even painful history which one would like to forget. It reminds one of the foundational principles on which one is based and can be a means of constant challenge to renew the old vigor and the zeal of the early beginnings. The author refers to the fact that the "household" of God is built upon "the foundation of the apostles and prophets," a phrase not likely to have been used by Paul, nor perhaps even in vogue during the lifetime of the first generation Christians. Paul himself refers to Jesus as *the* foundation of the church (see 1 Corinthians 3:11).

There are several points which deserve attention in this portion of the writing. The Gentiles are reminded of the greatness of God's act in Christ by this description of their state before Christ came. There is, however, no longer a distinction between Jew and Gentile; both are called together into the new creation of the church. And the Greek verb denotes a constant and continuous "remembering." In verse 14 the author refers to "the dividing wall of hostility." Commentators have argued over this figure, for it is somewhat difficult to understand exactly the background for the expression. Some take it to mean the dividing wall in the temple in Jerusalem which separated the court of the Gentiles from the inner portion reserved only for Jews. An inscription has been found which warned Gentiles that they would be killed if they dared to venture beyond that point.

Others have argued that the dividing wall refers to the "hedge of the law" which protected God's people and gave them special privileges and set them apart from all others. Still others refer to the gnostic beliefs of "walls" which divided God from the created world. Whatever the exact background, it is clear that this writer views the old wall of hostility, both between God and humanity and between human beings, as being done away in the act of Christ.

What has occurred has brought the Gentiles and the Jews together with a common goal, dedicated to the same Lord. The hostility has, therefore, come to an end. The Greek here is again important. It reads "having killed the hostility" by means of the cross. That which caused the enmity between God and humanity and between people has not simply come to an end; it has been killed!

Another verse which has caused great debate is verse 20. There are two points of interest to be noted here. First, there is the reference to the "apostles and prophets" (which we have already mentioned in another connection). There is not really much problem with "apostles," those in the early church who were given special pride of place because of their early relationship with Jesus, or someone who had witnessed a special appearance of Jesus for the purpose of designating that one to a special assignment (as with Paul). But the reference here to "prophets" has caused some debate. Does the term refer to the Old Testament prophets whose writings were believed to have foreshadowed the coming of God's Messiah? Or does the term refer to the Christian prophets of the early church who were considered only second in importance to the apostles (see 1 Corinthians 12:28)? In all probability the latter meaning is to be preferred since the emphasis here is upon the church as a new entity in itself surpassing the old era of Judaism.

The second problem in the interpretation of this verse lies in the figure used to describe Jesus. Most translations call him the "chief cornerstone." The word used in the Greek text, however, does not really mean a cornerstone, but rather it denotes a "keystone." In favor of the idea of the cornerstone is the reference to the apostles and prophets as being the "foundation." The cornerstone then would be the central and focal point of the foundation, making Christ, therefore, still the crucial part of the establishment of the church. On the other hand, the figure of the "keystone" would emphasize the topmost part of the structure, the one piece that has to fit exactly to hold the entire building together. And since the emphasis has been in this section on bringing the Jews and Gentiles together into one structure (and in the writing as a whole to unite or bind all things together), this would lend emphasis to what holds them together. Whichever figure one chooses, the point is nonetheless clear. It is Christ who makes the church what the church is!

There is yet another interpretative problem in verse 21. The translation reads, "the whole structure." But again this is not exactly what the Greek says. The literal translation is "every building." Understood with this meaning, the term would probably be a reference to the fact that the church is composed of various individual churches and would emphasize one of the key ideas of the book of Ephesians, namely, that the church is a universal organism composed of parts from many places and from many peoples. This interpretation makes sense with what follows: in Christ every part of the church is joined together and "grows into a holy temple in the Lord." This is precisely the emphasis of the author of this treatise.

And lastly, there is here also another figure which is found frequently toward the end of the first century A.D. It is the idea that the people of God have formed a new temple (see John 2:19ff.; Revelation 21:22ff.) and that God's Presence can be seen in this new "building." There is the emphasis especially in the Johannine literature that God is not to be limited by time or space or geographical locale. His Presence is to be with his people; God's dwelling will be among his people, and there the Spirit will be active giving growth to the church and sustaining power to its members. Something like this seems to be included here in this passage in Ephesians.

Ephesians 3:1-13: This passage begins with the words "For this reason," but it fails to continue immediately its line of thought. Instead, the flow of thought is interrupted by a long digression depicting the centrality of the apostle Paul in God's plan to unite Jew and Gentile in Christ. The original line of thought is picked up again in verse 14. Looking at the passage only casually, the interpreter could very well view verses 2-13 as an intrusion into the text. In fact, there are some commentators who argue that these verses were indeed added at a later time. But on close examination of the context, it appears that the author has carefully and very deliberately set these verses into this setting to emphasize a point.

Those who argue for the Pauline authorship of Ephesians look to this passage as proof positive that Paul did in fact write this document. They are also somewhat embarrassed by the tone of the passage which seems quite boastful to the one hearing or reading the material. It is not impossible for Paul to have written such a passage, however. He certainly was not above making his own case (see 2 Corinthians 11:21ff.) nor above self-effacing statements (see 1 Corinthians 15:9-10). The epistle to the Galatians is heavily interlaced with self-assertions and personal defense. But all of these passages must be understood against the backdrop of the historical circumstances against which Paul wrote. While Paul is certainly not above defending himself or asserting himself, he does so in the genuine letters only when attacked personally or when his teaching has been called into question.

The comments here in Ephesians, however, do not seem to reflect that kind of background. One of the commentators on this epistle has summarized this passage very well.

> Those who understand the epistle as post-Pauline see this as a device, common in ancient times, by which the actual writer disclaims all credit for what he writes and ascribes it to the one he seeks to represent. This writer feels that he is merely reproducing what he has learnt from Paul. His intention is to convey Paul's teaching to men of his own day, as if Paul himself were writing to them from prison, as he had done to the Colossians.[1]

If, indeed, someone else is writing these words to impress upon his readers that the words contained herein are basically the words of Paul (we remember the number of passages taken from Paul's letters), this passage begins to make better sense, and the explanation as to how Paul could have said these things about himself without provocation can be understood much more easily. And this passage does seem to reflect a period of history when Paul is beginning to be recognized as the real founder of the Gentile church, that is, humanly speaking.

The writer depicts Paul as a "prisoner of Jesus Christ." Most interpreters take this to mean that he is depicting Paul as being in prison because of Jesus Christ—and this may well mean exactly that.

---

[1] C. Leslie Mitton, *Ephesians,* The New Century Bible (Greenwood, S.C.: The Attic Press, 1976), p. 117.

But it is also possible that the phrase could indicate that Paul was Jesus Christ's prisoner. That would make good sense and may be the intended connotation.

Verse 2 is another of those interesting passages in this document. Many have argued that it would be strange indeed for Paul to say, "assuming that you have heard" about me and my work. If the letter were by Paul and to churches in an area where he was known, a comment like this would be quite surprising, if not out of place. But if this writing were directed to a time after Paul, and if it is an attempt of some kind to make Paul's life and thought known to a generation that had only heard of him as a figure of the past, this comment would be quite in order and not surprising at all.

Also we find another of those curious little differences between Paul's letters and this one. In Colossians Paul is given a task to perform; the Greek word used is *oikonomia*. Here in Ephesians, however, *oikonomia* designates the plan of God given through his grace. And it is the grace which is given to Paul! In this passage one also hears echoes of Galatians as well as Colossians. The emphasis is again on God's plan to have all people, Gentiles as well as Jews, as part of the ultimate purpose of Christ's work.

One approaches in this passage one of the most famous and well-known of all New Testament quotations. It is a magnificent description of what God can do, has done, and will continue to do. He has offered to the world the "unsearchable riches of Christ." The word translated "unsearchable" has the literal meaning of "not tracked out," and it came to mean "inscrutable" (as in Romans 11:33) or perhaps "fathomless." The meaning is that God's riches are so many that there is an unending supply which we can never exhaust.

Then in verse 10 there is the startling statement that not only is Paul called upon to bear the glad tidings of God's grace, but also now it is the church which is to be the means of carrying on the proclamation of those riches of God. And the wisdom of God has an infinite number of nuances and directions which continue to surprise and amaze as the revelation of God continues to be made. The New Testament writers really did believe that the highest revelation of God had been made in Christ, but they did not believe that God's revelation had therefore ceased or that there was no more to be revealed to the human race. One is reminded of that famous saying from the Gospel of John (which comes from this same period in the history of the church), that "when the Spirit of truth comes, he will guide you into all the truth" (John 16:13).

This truth is to be conveyed to the "principalities and powers in the heavenly places." Again there is some discussion about the exact meaning of this phrase. It is possible that the term could refer to the "angels in heaven," but it is unlikely that they would not already know these aspects of God's grace. It is more likely that these "powers" represent the forces of evil which were basically responsible at the spiritual level for the death of the Messiah. In doing away with him these powers felt that they had defeated God's plan and destroyed the last great hope for the redemption of the world. But they were mistaken. Not only had God raised his Messiah from the realm of death and exalted him to his own right hand, but the power of the resurrection had also been given to the church. And in the church it may be concretely seen that the power of sin and evil has been broken; the world is being reconciled to God. It is a marvelous and yet frightening description of what the church is to be.

Because of Christ's action, the church is able to do these things since God is now accessible to people. He is not hidden, far-off, distant, or uncaring. No matter if the world does the worst it can do, one is challenged not to become "cowardly." The worst that the world can do has already been shown to be ineffective and futile.

Ephesians 3:14-21: We come now to one of the most famous and beautiful of all the passages in this treatise. It is very difficult to do justice to this letter in its entirety in attempting to point out its meaning, for so often in reading this literary (as well as religious) masterpiece one is overwhelmed by the beauty and majesty of its words and message by simply reading it. It is even more difficult to comment on this segment, for I feel that anything which can be said would detract from its beauty. One, nevertheless, must attempt to note several points.

First of all, there is the argument that this passage is a liturgical passage. This point is argued by those who see in this writing a background in the liturgy and worship of the early church. It is sometimes specifically suggested that these words may have been used after a person had just been baptized. I find that unlikely, but the passage is quite appropriate for just that setting.

The setting here is not one of prayer but one of doing honor to a king or ruler. Kneeling was not the usual way of praying, especially in the Jewish background where prayer was done while standing. There is also in verses 14-15 a play on words that is impossible to bring out in an English translation, and through this device the text emphasizes the unity between God as Father and the church as containing his children. (The word "father" is *pater;* the word for family is *patria*.) It is interesting to note also that the term "every family" seems to suggest a collecting together of separate groups into one larger whole. We have seen that the emphasis in Ephesians is on the unity of the church in a universal sense, and there have been other instances in this epistle where individual churches have been depicted by other figures of speech. The word "church" in this writing is reserved by the author always for the idea of the church universal. And the church has been "named," that is, constituted by God.

The author again points out that the Christian is different because the Spirit strengthens the "inner man" through the fact that Christ is dwelling in their hearts through faith. Verse 18 has been a favorite homiletical playground for Christian preachers through the years. Some have argued that the four dimensions cited here are somehow related to the four points of the cross, or some similar argument. But this kind of interpretation is fanciful and foreign to the text. The terms are probably simply another way of describing the "unsearchable" (as discussed in verse 8).

One final point needs to be emphasized. As important as knowledge is, not simply to the gnostics but to the Christians also, the characteristic of the Christian life is not knowledge but love. The way one is filled with the fullness of God is to "know the love of Christ which surpasses knowledge." (See the discussion on Colossians 1:9-14.)

This section is now concluded with a doxology which again emphasizes the theme of the entire first three chapters: The gifts and gracious acts of God have been freely given to all who will accept in faith. These gifts are far beyond anything which human knowledge or power could either accomplish or even comprehend infinitesimally. Again the outlook is for a long time to come, "all generations." "Now to him who by the power at work within us is able to do far more abundantly than all that we ask or think, to him be glory in the church and in Christ Jesus to all generations, for ever and ever. Amen."

Ephesians 4:1-16: There seems to be a definite break between chapter 3 and chapter 4. Some interpreters like to think of this as being an example, found in many of Paul's letters, of the division of the body of the letter into two parts, one doctrinal and one ethical. But while this pattern is found in some of Paul's letters, he never really draws that rigid a distinction between doctrine and practice. In

Paul's thought these elements interpenetrate one another and are both considered essential to the Christian life. The pattern, however, may well have influenced the basic structure of this writing since the author of Ephesians is so intent upon reproducing Paul's words and ideas.

In the chapters which precede this section the author has argued in magnificent language for the greatness of God's sovereign plan for the universe, centering in the work of the Messiah. This plan is to be continued and epitomized in the church which is considered to be the continuing instrument for the work of the Christ as it is "energized" by the Spirit.

Beginning with chapter 4, the emphasis begins to turn to a more direct challenge to the church to be and to become what was intended for it in the plan of God kept secret until the time of the Christ. There is in this section then a challenge not only to the church as a corporate body but also to the individual persons who make up that body. The people of God, as depicted in the New Testament writings, are never simply submerged into a large mass to become a group composed of robots, each looking, thinking, and acting the same. Neither is the church composed of individual personalities, each one "doing one's thing," as the popular expression has it. Within the church there is a challenge both to heighten the unity of the larger group and at the same time to sharpen the individuality of each member. The group is to be a support to the individual, and the individual is to use one's talents to contribute to the well-being of the group.

The beginning of this section (4:1) is in the main almost identical with the words of Romans 12:1. The author exhorts his hearers and readers to "lead a life worthy" of their calling. The emphasis here is upon the fact that they have been "called," chosen by God to do a special task in his service. (This kind of thought is quite reminiscent of the old prophetic call for the prophets of the Old Testament.)

The characteristics of one who has accepted this "call" are to be "lowliness and meekness." Quite often persons in the church interpret these qualities to designate something like a "doormat" philosophy: True Christians are the ones who allow anyone and everyone to "walk over" them, to use them in any way. But the terms do not indicate such an interpretation, and neither do the lives of the New Testament personalities (Jesus, Paul, Peter, John, etc.) reflect such an understanding. The terms are more reflective of a person who is totally dedicated to the call one has received, and this person has committed his or her entire strength and being toward the goals of the

One who has issued the call, to accomplish his aims, to call attention to him and his work, not to call attention to oneself.

It is interesting also to note that the writer is very realistic. He seems to understand that when different people make a commitment to God, there will probably be some differences of opinion and thus "friction" among the people; so he urges "forbearing one another in love, eager to maintain the unity of the Spirit in the bond of peace." The word translated "eager" is really a verb in the Greek which means "being zealous, hastening." One is to work with zeal at the sometimes difficult task of getting along with all people, not the least of whom may be one's Christian brothers and sisters!

The reason for this admonition stems from the author's view of the church. There is to be one "body," and we are already familiar with the figure that the church is the "body of Christ," which is activated and infused with one Spirit. This understanding of the church rests upon the fact that there is one God who has called all people together to have fellowship with him and with each other for the well-being of all.

Most students of the Bible are familiar with the words found in verses 5-6: ". . . one Lord, one faith, one baptism, one God and Father of us all, who is above all and through all and in all." Some interpreters confess bewilderment at some aspects of this passage. Why are some motifs and ideas central to the early church (such as the Lord's Supper) omitted and these specifically singled out? In all probability the list here is simply one meant to emphasize the author's main point, namely, the unity of the church founded on the plan and purpose of the one God. These other items are the ones which simply came to his mind in the attempt to make his point.

Two points can be mentioned, however, as perhaps significant for our understanding of the passage. It is interesting to note that in this passage "faith" seems to mean something different from the understanding usually found for the word. Here it comes very close to the idea of designating a content of proper and correct theological thinking. This understanding of faith is also reflected in the Pastoral Epistles, almost unanimously agreed to be documents from the latter part of the first century A.D.

The second item for discussion is the meaning of "all" in verse 6. From the Greek it is possible to interpret the word in at least two ways. It could be viewed as a neuter gender, meaning "all things." This interpretation would emphasize the work of God in Christ to bring all the loose ends of the universe together. But the word could also be a masculine, rendering the meaning "all people." This would emphasize the work of God in Christ among the members of the human race, i.e., between Jews and Gentiles as the author has argued previously. It is difficult to make a choice here, because the author has laid the foundation in chapters 1-3 for either of these meanings. It just may well be that he intended for the reader to understand it both ways, in its broadest possible meaning.

The next portion of this passage, verses 7-16, is highly debated among interpreters and consists of only one sentence in the Greek! The basic question is with regard to the "descent" of Christ referred to in verse 9. Some scholars have argued that the "descent" here was intended to imply the descent of Christ into the world, i.e., his incarnation. Others see here a reference to the later idea in the early church which held that Jesus descended into "hell" or the place of the dead after his death on the cross. A New Testament illustration of this is found in 1 Peter 4:6. There is also another interpretation which sees in this passage a reference to the descent of the Spirit at Pentecost.[2]

The context of the passage does not seem to call for such elaborate schemes of interpretation as some scholars have argued. Verse 7 sets the tone for the entire thought: "grace was given to each of us." For what purpose? The purpose has already been set out in 4:1-6, the unity of the church and its development and growth. Therefore the argument over who belonged to the "host of captives" could be answered most logically and most simply: Christians. The controversy over the meaning of verse 9 would then most logically and simply be settled by assuming that the meaning is of Christ coming to the earth and then being raised to the right hand of God. He has given "gifts to men" in that he has called them to be part of his church and has equipped them to do various duties and tasks.

The list given here of "gifts" distributed to the people of the church reminds the reader immediately of Paul's argument to the people of Corinth (see I Corinthians 12). There are, however, in this list two groups not found in Paul's writings, namely, evangelists and pastors. In the time of Paul it seems to have been assumed that part of the apostle's task was that of being an evangelist. One recalls that Paul himself, even though carefully guarding his claim to the status of "apostle," did actually do the work of an evangelist. The work seems to be that of making the Good News known in the world. But now at

[2] See Introduction and commentary by George B. Caird, *Paul's Letters from Prison: Ephesians, Philippians, Colossians, Philemon,* The New Clarendon Bible (Oxford: Oxford University Press, 1976), pp. 73-78.

this later time when the apostles were past, the term "evangelist" seems to have been used for this "gift."

The other word, pastors (literally, shepherds), is only used here in the New Testament in the sense of an office in the church. The person in this capacity appears to be one whose primary duties were directed toward the people in the local congregation, in much the same way that we use the term "pastor" today.

But all these persons, who obviously were believed to have special status in the church order of the day, were granted these gifts for one purpose—for "building up the body of Christ." These people will assist and lead all Christians to the "unity of the faith and of the knowledge of the Son of God." The matter is one of growing in understanding so that Christians will be "mature" and will not be misled by false and deceptive teachings. The likelihood of being deceived by false teaching was always possible even from the very beginning of the Christian church, but much more so as the church grew and progressed, for there were numerous people who claimed to have new and correct interpretations for the Christian to follow. The warning here is for the Christian to become mature so as not to be led astray by false teaching.

It is clear from this passage that the Christian life is to be one characterized by growth. One is not transformed immediately nor does one ever understand all there is of the richness of God's plan and purpose. But one is challenged to "grow up in every way into him who is the head, into Christ" (v. 15).

Ephesians 4:17-24: This passage begins a long section in which the Christians are directly challenged to live the new life available to them. The wording seems to imply that the people who are being addressed had been Gentiles. The author charges that before Christ the Gentile world had been characterized by "futility." This word signifies a lack of meaning or purpose or direction. The condition results because they had deliberately chosen to remain in that state of existence. As a result they had become callous, unfeeling of others, and totally selfish, which led to perversion in all areas of human life but especially in the area of sexual relations.

The biblical writers never viewed sexual relations as evil; rather, they looked upon this relationship as one of the most joyous gifts which God had given to the human race. It is a part of the natural order, and as such it is to be used and enjoyed. But human beings, as they are apart from God, can and do use sexual activity simply as a means of self-gratification, using other persons for their own pleasure. But this perverted usage is not a part of God's plan for this gift. Therefore, very strong restrictions are placed upon sexual activity in the biblical revelation, not to demonstrate that sexual activity is wrong but to regulate it and keep it from being abused. When such abuse occurs, this leads to more and more self-gratification. People become "greedy to practice *every kind* of uncleanness" (italics added). The pagan world of that time was notorious for such an attitude toward sexual relations. It is, to a great degree, analogous to our time!

The writer, however, sharply challenges the Christians. "You did not so learn Christ!" The term "learn Christ" is a curious one, but the meaning seems to be that what they had heard about Jesus and were taught in him did not contain this kind of life-style. The Christian is urged again to put off the old nature, leave behind the old life-style, and to put on a new nature "created after the likeness of God." The emphasis is on the fact that God creates this new nature, and there is a large difference between this new nature and the old nature apart from God.

Ephesians 4:25–5:2: The exhortation to right living continues with an appeal for honesty in dealings with one another. There is always a need for this Christian virtue, for too often personal relationships and individual lives have been destroyed because of a lack of honesty. The same is true today. No longer is "our word our bond," but words today are cheap vehicles to get us what we want or out of trouble or the like.

An interesting aspect of this passage is that which deals with anger. Quite often we have been told that anger has no place in a Christian's life, but this writer says that one should be angry. The Greek literally says, "Keep on being angry, but stop sinning"—a curious comment. Current in our understanding of God's love is a strong element which argues that God cannot be wrathful or vengeful because these qualities stem from anger, and anger is an unacceptable human emotion. It is true that anger is not number one on the list of attributes which we usually enumerate in describing God, but anger is definitely in the biblical list. It is there because human beings have been given a freedom by God to reject him, his ways, his offers of redemption. People have the right to say "NO!" to God. They sin, and they hurt other people, especially the people who attempt to practice goodness and kindness. These people, according to the Scriptures, cause God quite justifiably to be angry, and there seems to be a place for the proper kind of human anger as well. Being angry at injustice, immorality, unfairness, or just sin in general is not something to be diminished. This anger must be exercised, however, with great caution so as not to become a means of venting one's own hostility. There can be, therefore, positive ways of expressing anger. The Christian's task is to find these ways—but to stop sinning in the process! Anger should never become an all-consuming passion (see v. 26*b*).

The people are challenged to refrain from stealing, from speaking evil (probably a reference to degrading one's neighbors), and from every kind of "malice." These are not part of the Christian life-style, and no one who bears the name of true Christian will be characterized by such activity.

The first two verses of chapter 5 then give a challenge for those who are a part of the Christian church: constantly "be imitators of God" and constantly "walk in love." The Christian life is not a "one-shot deal," but it is a constant and sometimes painful struggle to become what God intends us to be. The life of Christ sets an example of self-giving concern and love for others that his followers should emulate.

These two verses (5:1-2) form a vital connecting link between 4:25-32 and 5:3ff.

Ephesians 5:3-20: At this point the writer of Ephesians returns to present another section dealing with moral problems which Christians must shun. It is interesting to note in connection with this passage that there are several lists of vices contained within the New Testament writings; and while the lists are different at various points, there is one "sin" which is most frequently mentioned. It leads the list here beginning at 5:3.

The English translations usually identify this sin simply as "immorality." The word itself, however, denotes more precisely immorality in the sexual sphere. And it is quite probable that all three words in this verse have reference to some form of sexual aberration. These kinds of vices, so common in the pagan world, were not even "to be named" among Christians!

Verse 4 also presents some problem of interpretation because the challenge here is not to speak of such things, and the author even warns against "levity." Too many persons have interpreted this as an admonition against laughter of any kind in the Christian life. The word does not in this context denote humor as such, but the meaning probably carries the idea of crude and distasteful humor dealing primarily with sexual matters. Then there follows the admonition to give "thanks," to some a puzzling turn. But in the context here it seems clear enough that the author is challenging the Christians to keep sexual matters in proper perspective. Since sexuality was given by God to the human race as a gift, it should be perceived and exercised and even thought about in the most respectful way. Giving thanks to God for this good gift would be the proper and appropriate manner to understand and accept it, not by cheap and filthy thoughts and actions.

The challenges in verses 6-7 not to be deceived or to associate with evil people are again in the Greek a reminder to be warned constantly and continuously about such people. Exactly who these people were remains a mystery, but some interpreters think that the reference (arising from this specific context) may be to gnostic-type persons who were arguing that since the physical body does not count, only the spirit, one could do anything with one's body. The people are reminded, however, that this kind of activity carries with it a judgment.

The duty of the Christian is not only to abstain from participation in such practices but also actively to "expose" them. There is a problem with this word in that the meaning and intent are questioned by some commentators. Some have argued that the "exposing" takes place within the Christian community, i.e., people pointing at the sins of the other people within the Christian group. There is also a problem as to the exact meaning of the word "expose." It can have the idea of "convict," "rebuke," or even "to show up." Therefore, one can see that there is some problem. But the context here seems to dictate that the meaning is simple enough. Christians are not simply to abstain from sin, but actually to expose it as sin wherever it occurs, either within the Christian community or outside it. One cannot be neutral in this world. One must either belong to the light or to the darkness; there is no middle ground. It is, therefore, the Christian's duty to demonstrate, by what one does or does not do, the difference between the light and the darkness. What one does or does not do will demonstrate the difference between God's way and the world's way, and this will assist people in making the choice (see verse 13).

In verse 14 the reader is alerted to the fact that a quotation, perhaps from Scripture, is forthcoming. But there is no Old Testament Scripture for this quotation, unless it is a reworked form of Isaiah 60:1. Most scholars take this as a part of a Christian hymn (see

Ephesians 5:18-19), perhaps even one associated with the baptismal rite. But certainty cannot be reached on this matter. The point seems to be that the one who has been raised with Christ has light. And this light enables one to walk in the proper manner as the author emphasizes in verses 15-20.

To be in the light of Christ will make one "wise," able to see the right and able to see the consequences of failing to do the right! The curious reference to becoming "drunk with wine" seems to be set within the context of Christian worship (see vv. 18-20). The community is urged not to become drunk, but the problem is in knowing exactly when, where, or how the author intends the admonition to be understood. Some have argued that this is a reference to the pagan practice of using alcohol (or drugs) to enable one to have mystical experiences or visions. This could well be a residual problem from the paganism from which these people were called, or it could be a reference to an "enlightened gnostic" teaching.

Paul had also experienced the same kind of problem with the church at Corinth where the more well-to-do members came to celebrate the Lord's Supper early (the earliest celebration of this rite in all probability was a full-scale meal, sometimes called an *agape,* or love feast). By the time the poorer people had arrived, most of the food was gone and some even had become drunk! Paul, needless to say, was not happy about that (see 1 Corinthians 11:17ff.). The circumstances here could have been similar to Paul's problem with the Corinthians, but the tone and setting seem to indicate something else. The Greek says "Stop getting drunk"! It seems plausible that the same people who were advocating sexual freedom may well also have been advocating freedom with regard to the use of wine even in the context of the worshiping community. The author of Ephesians wishes to set that misconception aright, for the overuse of this item leads directly into "debauchery," that which is characteristic of "unsaved" behavior. The author urges the Christian to be filled with the Spirit, not spirits!

It is perhaps wise to pause for a moment at this point to examine the term "because the days are evil," found in verse 16. There are some interpreters who have taken this to be an indication of the return of Christ, and it is possible to interpret the phrase in such a way. But it is perhaps much more probable to understand the term differently. In the first place, there has not been and will not be any reference otherwise to the expected return of Christ in this treatise. Secondly, the context here is not conducive to that kind of interpretation. The author has been urging the Christian people to refrain from the old ways of paganism, to work in the light, to shun evil deeds and ways. The word used for "evil" in this verse is similar and related to the one used before for "sexual impurity." The meaning of the term, then, seems to be something like our "the times are evil," i.e., moral standards are so low that no one really thinks about the evil going on.

Finally, it should be noted that there is here a glimpse into how the early Christian worship was conducted. The people are to address each other with "psalms and hymns and spiritual songs." These are to be done in all sincerity, "with all your heart."

Ephesians 5:21–6:9: This section of Ephesians has obviously been structured after a similar passage in Colossians (see Colossians 3:18–4:1). Paul in Colossians had discussed the relationship between husbands and wives, parents and children, and slaves and masters. The emphasis there had been on the slave-master relationship owing to the problems related to Onesimus and his master, Philemon. In Ephesians the identical relationships are discussed and in the same order, but there has been a considerable shift of emphasis. By far the largest amount of space is reserved for the husband-wife motif, but if one reads the section carefully, it becomes very apparent that the husband-wife metaphor is only the foundation for a much more important matter for this writer. He uses this human relationship as an analogy for the relationship between Christ and the church. As such, the interpreter must beware lest too much be read into the husband-wife motif which is not determinative for life-style but is only a figure for a deeper reality in a different area entirely.

The entire section begins with an overall admonition to "be subject to one another out of reverence for Christ." The present tense again indicates a continuous action, and the verb indicates a strong degree of subordination. The meaning does not advocate the "doormat" philosophy, i.e., the Christian is to do anything and everything which someone may want. Rather, the "being subject" is within the church group itself, and, further, the subjection is always guided by the "fear" of Christ. Things which are out of line with the will of Christ are not to be done. The portrait here is of a group of people, committed to Christ and therefore to one another, who put one another's needs and well-being above their own. This has positive implications in all areas of life, but more especially in some than in others.

The first of these relates to the husband-wife relationship. We have already discussed the background for the assumptions of the social order in that period of history (see pp. 74-76), and it is not necessary to repeat that here. We are reminded that it was the accepted norm for husbands to be the ultimate authority in the home environment. This was their accepted order, and there has to be an accepted order for any society to exist peacefully and to have opportunity to progress. This understanding of the husband as "head of the house" lies at the foundation for the discussion in this treatise.

Wives are cautioned to be subject to their husbands, and husbands are commanded to "love [constantly and continuously] their wives." Throughout the entire section the husband-wife relationship (accepted as normal in those times but transformed under the new standards for Christians to treat all people, but especially each other, with new respect and dignity) is used as a pointer toward the understanding which the author has about the relationship of Christ and the church. This has been his primary concern throughout this entire document.

The section concludes with the curious words, "The mystery is a profound one, and I am saying that it refers to Christ and the church" (5:32). Literally in the Greek the reading is: "This mystery is great [or Great is this mystery], and I say [that it is] for the purpose of [unto, into, relates to] Christ and the church." The RSV translation is certainly not incorrect, but the simplest and most straightforward translation of the first clause is: "This mystery is great." The question remains as to its exact meaning.

Another problem with which interpreters wrestle here is the precise meaning of "mystery." In the other passages in this writing the word has indicated God's plan of uniting all things, especially the bringing together in one body the Jews and Gentiles. There seems to be no good reason to change the nuance of meaning here. The discussion of the husband-wife relationship has been brought to its full intent with the quotation from Genesis 2:24, about two people becoming one. This is a "mystery," that two separate people can become one. But this is also exactly what the church is: a group of different people from different backgrounds who have become one. The analogy is clear, and it is consistent with the remainder of the writing.

With that understanding of the word "mystery," the verse seems to take on clarity. The unity in the relationship between the husband and wife in marriage is somehow analogous to the relationship between Christ and the church in which God's plan is unity among all elements. This mystery (i.e., plan of God) is indeed great!

In 6:1-4 the corresponding section of Colossians (3:20-21) has been somewhat expanded. In this section the relationship between parents and children takes center stage. The author of Ephesians has expanded the discussion by adding the comment about the Fifth Commandment. Many commentators like to point out that this is not really the first commandment with a promise, but it is the first one with only a promise, and it is possible that the author intended the reader to understand his parenthetical comment in the sense "of primary importance." The meaning of this passage is quite similar to that in Colossians with the addition of the charge to the parents to rear the children "in the discipline and instruction of the Lord." This is not a passage which views the end of the world as imminent.

The last comments, as in Colossians, have to do with the slave-master relationship. The reader is referred to the discussion of that section of Colossians for comments about slavery in the ancient world and the Christian response to it (see p. 77). It is interesting to note here, however, that the emphasis among Christians is on mutual respect and responsibility for one another no matter what one's station in life. The master was to be concerned about the slave and his or her well-being, and the slave was to render the best service possible.

One may feel that this passage has little to say to the Christian situation today, but with closer thought one can see that there may be some real parallels. While we do not live in a time when people own other people as pieces of property (at least not in this century), slavery is deeper than simply owning as property another human being. There may yet be slavery even in our society though we may not recognize it as such. When people are economically dependent upon a job, for example, there is here a certain degree of "slavery" involved. Employers who exploit workers because of this economic dependence are, in fact, masters. And there are many unscrupulous masters in our world who attempt to force employees to do unethical and distasteful acts in order for the employee to keep his or her means of support or to be eligible for pay raises and/or promotions, or who promise rewards for good work and fail to keep their part of the bargain, or who take credit for ideas and work which others actually have done. Also we find employees each day who feel that they do not owe the employer anything for the money paid to them to perform a service. They become lazy, expecting all sorts of concessions and automatic (and large) pay raises without any increase in their own output or productivity.

To both of these groups the Scripture seems to speak rather

directly. The employer is to look out for the best interests of the employees, and the employee is to render faithful service to the employer. Both are called upon to be responsible and sensible people, for, as the author of Ephesians points out, "there is no partiality" with God.

Ephesians 6:10-20: Now in the final challenge and proclamation of hope combined here in this passage, the author completes his message to the church. The figure is that of a soldier prepared for battle with loins girded, proper footwear, and good protection. But the figure is not, as some have interpreted these verses, simply a defensive one. The "whole armor" includes offensive weapons as well, but the only offensive weapon which the Christian needs is the "word of God." It is definitely to be used in the battle against the forces of evil.

Verse 10 provides an interesting setting for this marvelous metaphor. The translation should read not "finally" but "from now on." This again gives to the book as a whole the strong impression that the battle is for a long time to come. This is reinforced by the use again of the present tense in the Greek, "keep on being empowered in the Lord." The author realizes that the fight will be long and difficult, but it can be fought and won through the power and might of God.

There is another interesting point made here. It is that the powers against which the Christian fights are not "flesh and blood," i.e., simply human adversaries. The real power of evil comes from without, a prevailing idea in that era of history. But the power of evil is manifested in and through human agents. There is in this universe a power or force of evil which transcends the human sphere but uses the arena of human history to exert its power and influence over the people of the world, especially the people of God. The struggle is, therefore, one which has both spiritual and physical aspects, and these aspects must be recognized and defended against by the Christian.

The people of God must be alert, because the operating principle of the powers of evil is deceit—deception. The author of Revelation understands that clearly also (see Revelation 13:1-4). The word translated "wiles" means a deliberate plan. As God had a "plan" for the world, so too do the forces of evil. God's plan is for the liberty of the created order; the forces of evil wish to destroy and enslave it. And the forces of evil will stop at nothing to accomplish their goals; to use a familiar term, "the ends justify the means" for their purposes.

The listing of the "armor" sometimes causes commentators some problems, because too many seek to understand the exact meaning of each term (righteousness, peace, etc.). Further, they seek to understand why other figures are not included! But to analyze the text in such a way, when such analysis is really unnecessary, kills the spirit of the writing. The author simply wishes to emphasize that when one is dedicated and committed to God, all the powers of the Spirit of God are available to that person in the fight against the powers and forces of evil. This battle is not one for the fainthearted nor will the victory be won easily. One of the keys is constant commitment and prayer.

The passage concludes with another reference to Paul as a prisoner, who is himself fighting against these same enemies. He urges their prayers that he be enabled to "proclaim the mystery of the gospel." It is the mystery of God's plan which we now understand more clearly, but which we shall probably never be able to understand fully. That would entail knowing fully the unsearchable wisdom of God who has given to the church and to the world the unsearchable riches of Christ.

Ephesians 6:21-24: We come now to the final verses of this magnificent writing. You are already aware of the close relationship between Colossians and this document. There are many passages which are very similar, and there are many words used which are identical. But most of the parallels are limited to three to five words used consecutively. Here, however, there are thirty-two words in order which are identical with the words of Colossians 4:7-8. Some argue that this proves that Paul wrote Ephesians; others argue that this proves that Paul did not write Ephesians! It has been the assumption of this study that an admirer of Paul is responsible for the writing, and that he attempted to use as much of Paul's own thought and words as possible. The key, however, seems to be that the historical circumstance reflected in Ephesians is from a time later than the period of the great apostle Paul.

Two other points can be mentioned. When one compares this passage with Colossians, one notices that Onesimus's name is omitted. Some use this as an argument both for and against the suggestion that Onesimus was the writer of Ephesians. And further, there is the direct mention of Tychicus. In this passage quoted basically from Colossians, Paul praises this man as a "beloved brother and faithful minister." Some have suggested that perhaps Tychicus was the writer of Ephesians. We simply do not know.

The benediction in verses 23-24 is simple but filled with beauty and dignity. The blessing is given to those who love the Lord with "love undying." The word means "not perishable," and the term probably implies a commitment that will not be shaken, either now or ever. This is the kind of commitment which distinguishes the Christian from the world and makes the church the church.

The problem of authorship regarding this New Testament writing pales into insignificance as one is overwhelmed by the majesty and depth of the understanding of God's act in Christ on behalf of the entire universe. Ephesians is truly a revelation of God; no matter who wrote it, this writer was magnificently inspired by a vision of God and by the Spirit of God in a mighty way.

7 Conclusion

Having examined now in more depth and detail the writings of Colossians and Ephesians, we can see much more clearly several of the points which were being discussed in chapters 1, 2, and 3. Both of these writings teach precisely and pointedly that the church owes its allegiance and very being to the act of God in and through Jesus the Christ. He is the Head of the church! Each of these books also makes it clear that Christ's essential being, while unique and related closely to God, is not as important for precise definition as what he came to do. For example, it was quite evident in Colossians that Christ was the one who *revealed* the nature of God to the world, for this seems to be the meaning of the term "image of God," found in that famous passage (1:15-20), but even that phrase carries with it the implication of a duty to be performed on behalf of the one who is being represented.

It is also clear that the primary work of Christ was the work of reconciliation. This reconciliation was not simply to bind up and to heal the broken relationship between God and the human race but to heal the relationship between human beings (e.g., Jew and Gentile, in Ephesians especially) and between God and the created order. The New Testament writers in general do not attempt to explain what happened or how it happened nor do the authors of Colossians and Ephesians in particular, but they all do proclaim that God has caused this marvelous work to be accomplished through his mighty action in Jesus the Christ. The reconciling work of Christ can bind all the broken relationships of the entire universe together.

This reconciliation which establishes a new relationship between the human race and God creates a new order of humanity, a new humanity, a new life-style. This life-style is different from that of the world, so different in fact that the world will be amazed to see it and, at the same time, threatened by it. The world and the forces of evil will do everything within their power (and that power is great) to destroy this new life. The victory, however, has already been won by Christ as God has raised him from the power of death to illustrate once and for all that the right kind of life is not affected by *real* death (i.e., being apart from God). Physical death is not to be feared, because the cessation of physical life does not alter the unity of the relationship which the believer has with God in Christ.

This revelation of God given through Christ and the power of this new life must be made known to all people everywhere. It is the responsibility, duty, and privilege of the church to take this message to the world. Unless the church proclaims to the world by word and deed the "unsearchable riches of Christ our Lord," the church is failing to be the church! The church was created to be *the* witness to the sovereignty of God in the universe and to the reconciling power of the work of Christ. This witness can be accomplished by various means and methods in different generations and in different circumstances, but in every generation and in every age the call is for the Christian and the church to demonstrate through love the power of God in the transformation process.

As for the matter of eschatological thinking, the New Testament documents do not all agree in terms of their outward expectations of what kind of events will constitute the "end." But all the documents do emphasize that the decisions which people make *now* for the direction of their lives and for the commitment of their lives to whatever "lord" they may choose do, have a note of finality about them. Human beings are responsible for the choices they make and for the choice of a master to whom they commit their lives. There does come an ultimate judgment. There are and will be those whose lives are dedicated to, committed to, and united with God, and there are and will be those whose lives are not so dedicated, committed, and united. To the New Testament writers the choice between these two alternatives was the most important decision a human being must make. They felt a responsibility to make this choice clear to all the people of the world.

When the world is still filled with evil and hatred, sickness, disease, starvation, loneliness, futile and directionless lives, and all the other ailments which afflict the universe in which we live, can the church and the Christian do less today?

Bibliography

General Books for Background

Efird, James M., *The New Testament Writings: History, Literature, and Interpretation.* Atlanta: John Knox Press, 1979.

Fitzmyer, Joseph, *Pauline Theology: A Brief Sketch.* Englewood Cliffs, N.J.: Prentice-Hall, Inc., 1967.

Furnish, Victor P., *The Moral Teaching of Paul.* Nashville: Abingdon Press, 1979.

Whiteley, D. E. H., *The Theology of St. Paul.* Philadelphia: Fortress Press, 1964.

Commentaries on Colossians and Ephesians

Caird, George B., *Paul's Letters from Prison: Ephesians, Philippians, Colossians, Philemon,* The New Clarendon Bible. Oxford: Oxford University Press, 1976.

Houlden, J. L., ed., *Paul's Letters from Prison: Philippians, Colossians, Philemon, and Ephesians,* Westminster Pelican Commentaries. Philadelphia: The Westminster Press, 1979. (Original edition 1970)

Scott, E. F., *The Epistles of Paul to the Colossians, to Philemon, and to the Ephesians.* The Moffatt New Testament Commentary. New York: Harper & Row, Publishers, Inc., 1930.

Thompson, G. H. P., *The Letters of Paul to the Ephesians, to the Colossians, and to Philemon.* The Cambridge Bible Commentary on the New English Bible. Cambridge: Cambridge University Press, 1967.

Commentaries on Colossians

Beare, Francis W., "The Epistle to the Colossians," *The Interpreter's Bible,* edited by G. A. Buttrick et al. Vol. 11. Nashville: Abingdon Press, 1955.

Bruce, F. F., "Commentary on the Epistle to the Colossians" in *Commentary on the Epistles to the Ephesians and the Colossians,* E. K. Simpson and F. F. Bruce. The New International Commentary on the New Testament. Grand Rapids, Mich.: Wm. B. Eerdmans Publishing Co., 1957.

Lohse, Eduard, *Colossians and Philemon,* translated by W. R. Poehlmann and R. J. Karris. Philadelphia: Fortress Press, 1971. Hermeneia. (Based on the Greek text.)

Martin, Ralph P., ed., *Colossians and Philemon.* The New Century Bible. Greenwood, S.C.: The Attic Press, 1974.

Moule, Charles F., *The Epistles of Paul the Apostle to the Colossians and to Philemon,* Cambridge Greek Testament Series. (Based upon the Greek text.) Cambridge: Cambridge University Press, 1957.

Commentaries on Ephesians

Barth, Markus, *Ephesians,* 2 vols. The Anchor Bible. Garden City, N.Y.: Doubleday & Co. Inc., 1974.

Beare, Francis W., "The Epistle to the Ephesians," *The Interpreter's Bible,* edited by G. A. Buttrick et al. Vol. 10. Nashville: Abingdon Press, 1953.

Mitton, Charles Leslie, *Ephesians,* The New Century Bible Series. Greenwood, S.C.: The Attic Press, 1977.

_____, *The Epistle to the Ephesians: Its Authorship, Origin and Purpose.* Oxford: The Clarendon Press, 1951. (A highly detailed and techincal work.)